Butterfly Flash

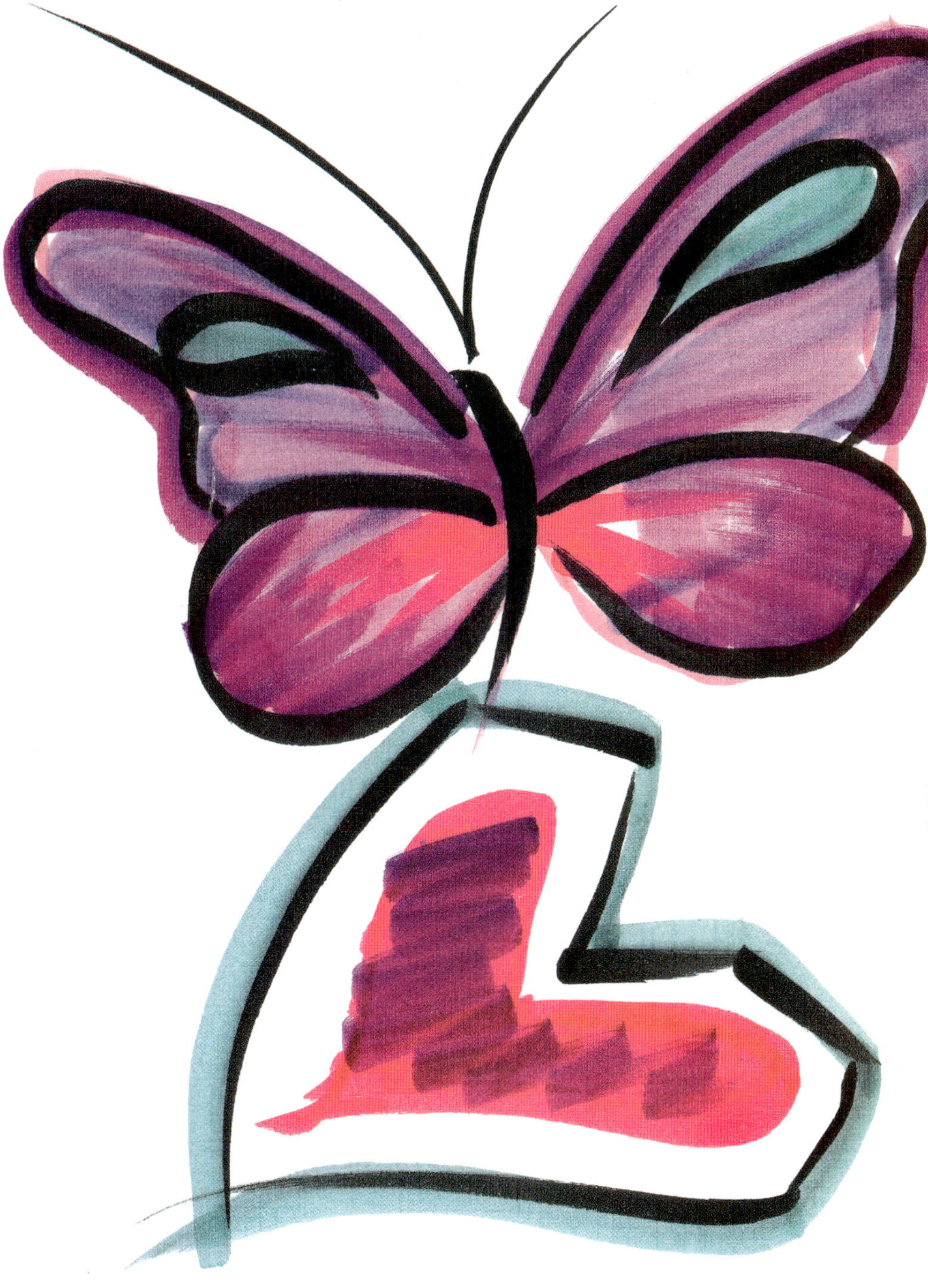

Spider Webb

Schiffer Publishing Ltd
4880 Lower Valley Road, Atglen, PA 19310 USA

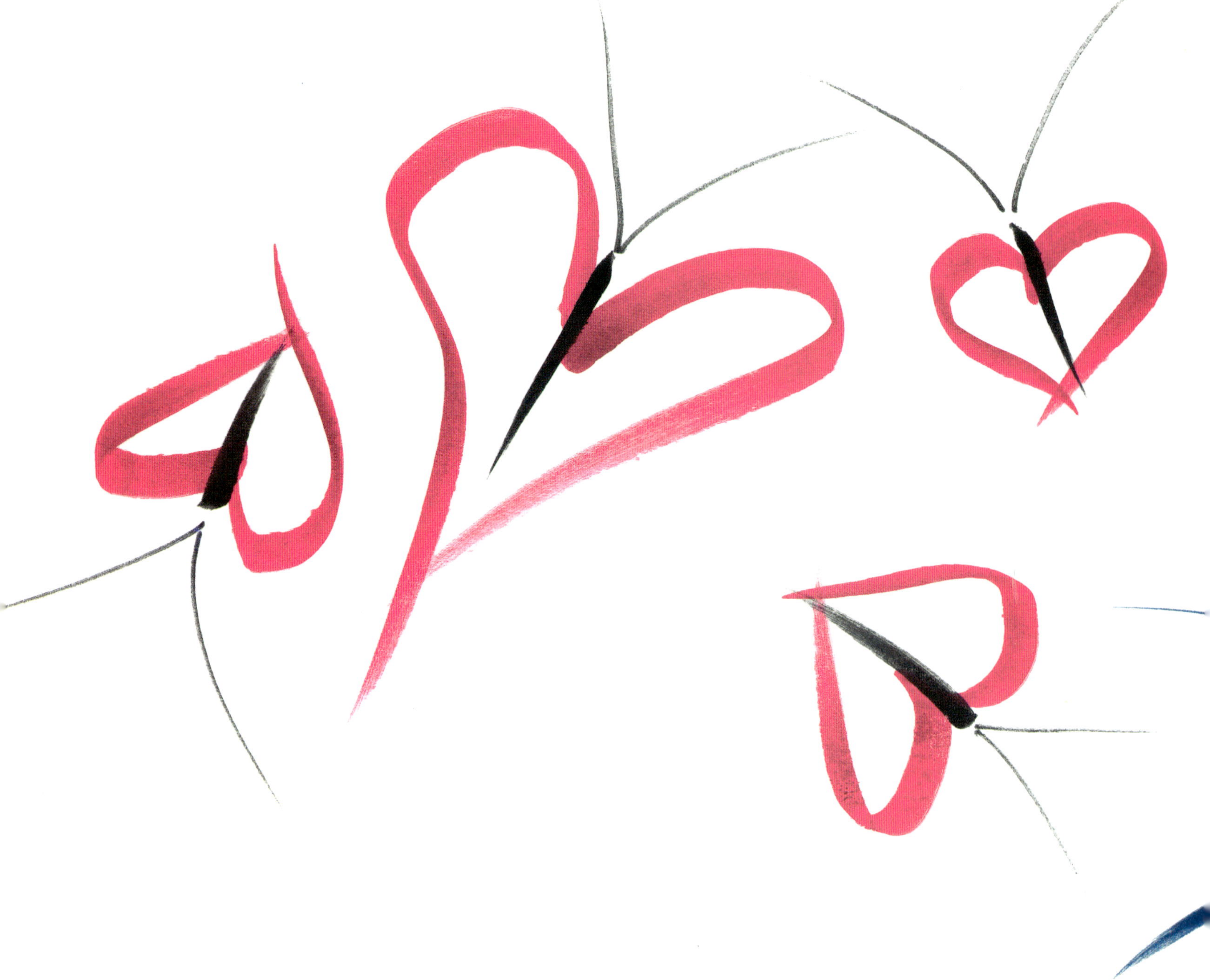

Library of Congress Control Number: 2001094055

Designed by Bonnie M. Hensley
Cover design by Bruce M. Waters
Typeset in Zurich Cn BT

ISBN: 0-7643-1505-6

Published by Schiffer Publishing Ltd.
4880 Lower Valley Road
Atglen, PA 19310
Phone: (610) 593-1777; Fax: (610) 593-2002
E-mail: Schifferbk@aol.com
Please visit our web site catalog at
www.schifferbooks.com

This book may be purchased from the publisher.
Include $3.95 for shipping. Please try your bookstore first.
We are always looking for people to write books on new and related subjects. If you have an idea for a book please contact us at the above address.
You may write for a free catalog.

In Europe, Schiffer books are distributed by
Bushwood Books
6 Marksbury Avenue
Kew Gardens
Surrey TW9 4JF England
Phone: 44 (0) 20-8392-8585; Fax: 44 (0) 20-8392-9876
E-mail: Bushwd@aol.com
Free postage in the UK. Europe: air mail at cost.

Dedication

To Pat and Mary Daley and to my old pal Quention Crisp.

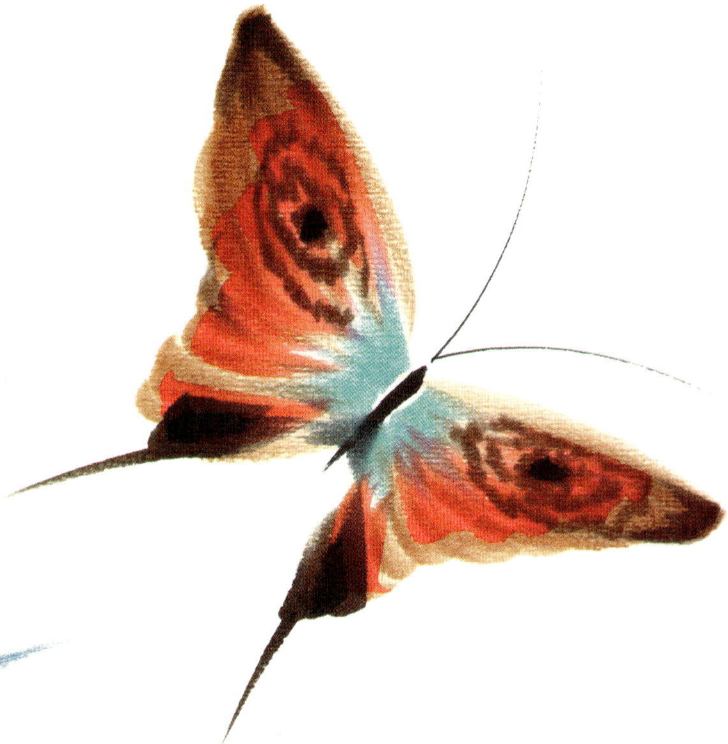

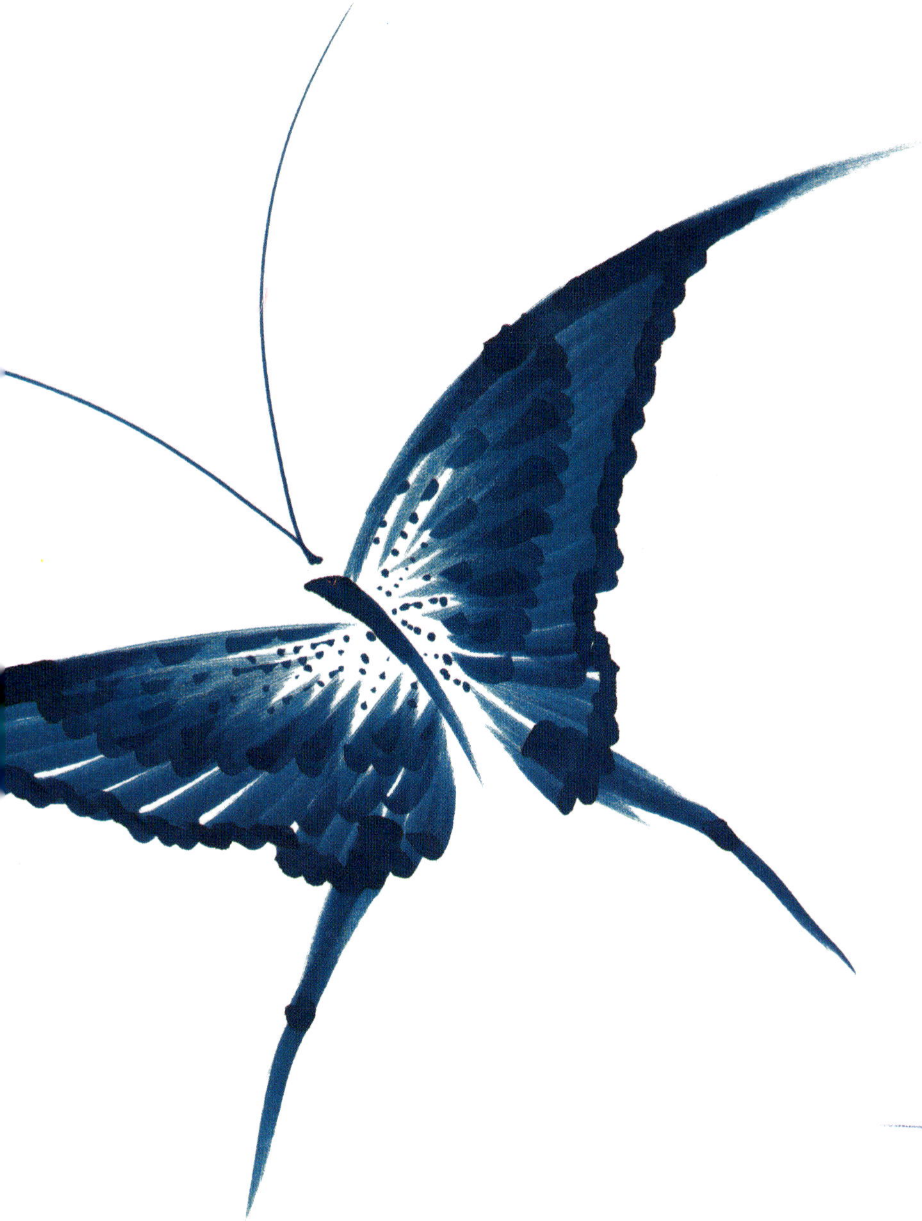

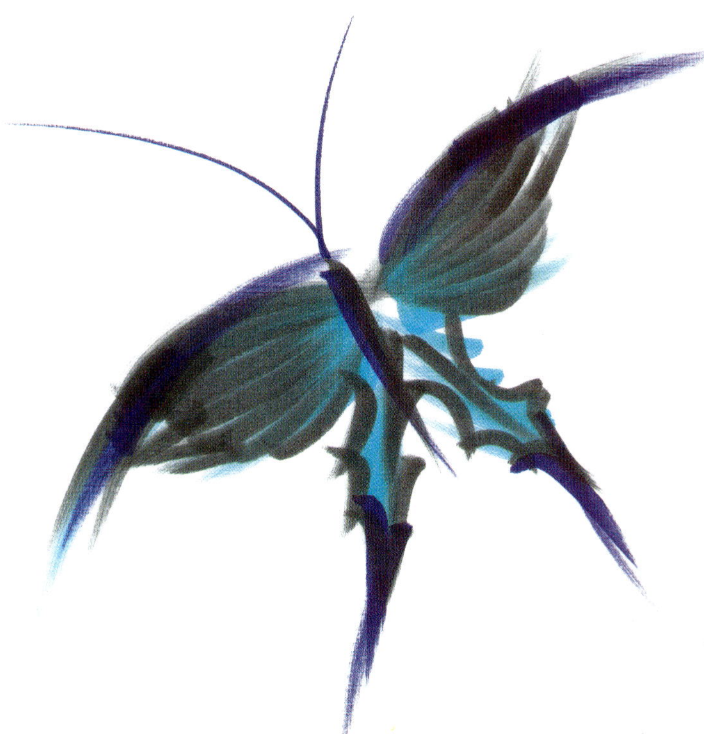

Preface

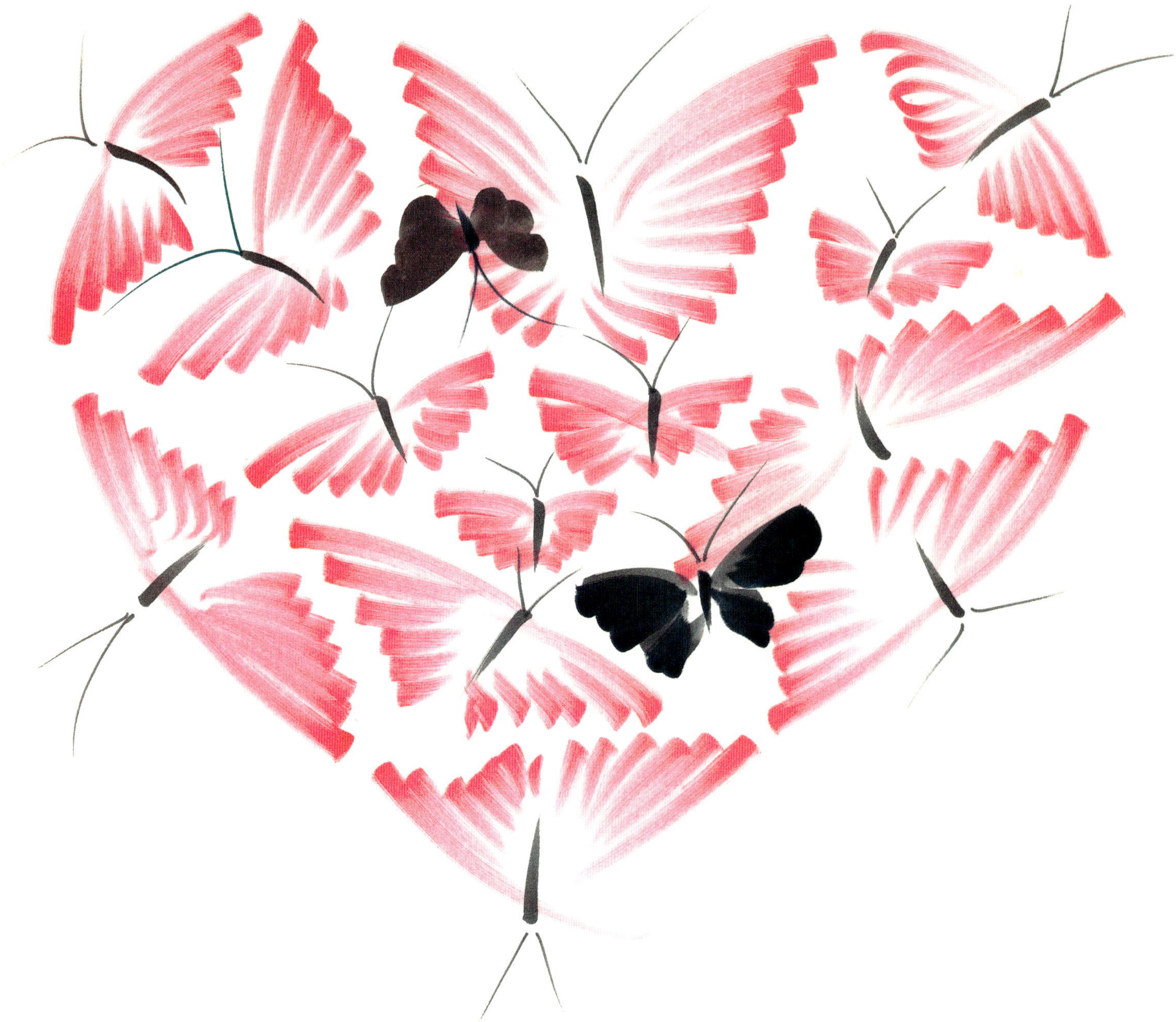

International tattoo artist, Spider Webb made a New Year's resolution to make 1999 the year of the butterfly. He wanted to paint 2,000 butterfly compostions for the year 2000.

He soon exceeded his goal.

"I thought it would be a big deal," he said. "That it would take a lot of time. I had over 2,000 by February. Then I just stopped counting and just kept doing them. I gave them away and sold a whole bunch of them. They've flown all over the world."

Webb's butterflies adorn innumerable canvases and countless sheets of art paper. He has painted butterflies on doors, on dividers, and painted butterflies floor-to-ceiling in his home.

"Butterflies represent rebirth and the whole metamorphism thing, freedom and all that," he says. "In the 1960s, they were part of the whole psychedelic thing."

Webb has his own butterfly tattoo on his body. Now his work will go on to inspire hundreds of other body artists. Every page in this book is a delightful amalgamation of fluttering butterflies, each unique and beautiful. Nature had a good head start, but she would have trouble keeping up with this prolific artist.

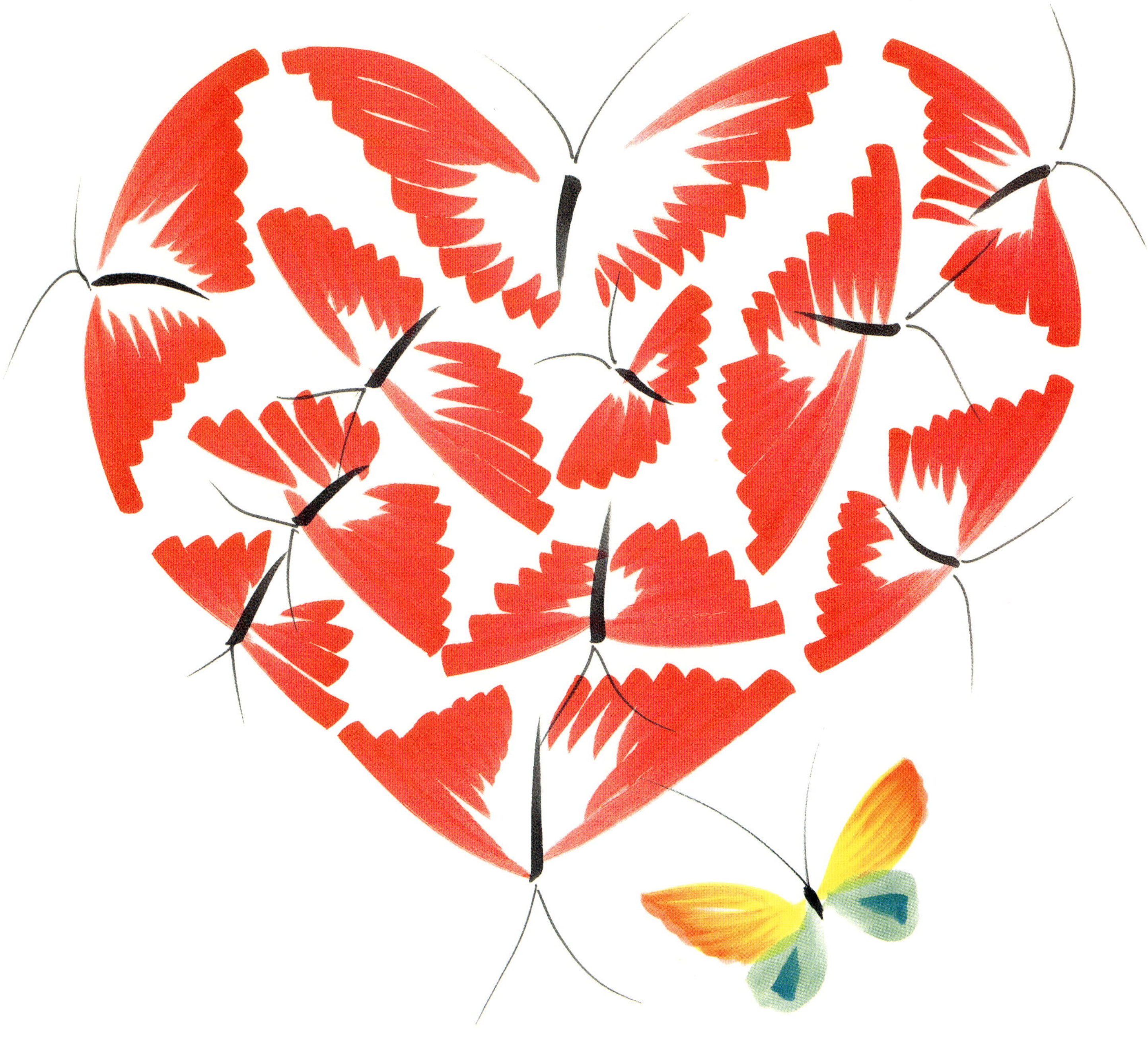

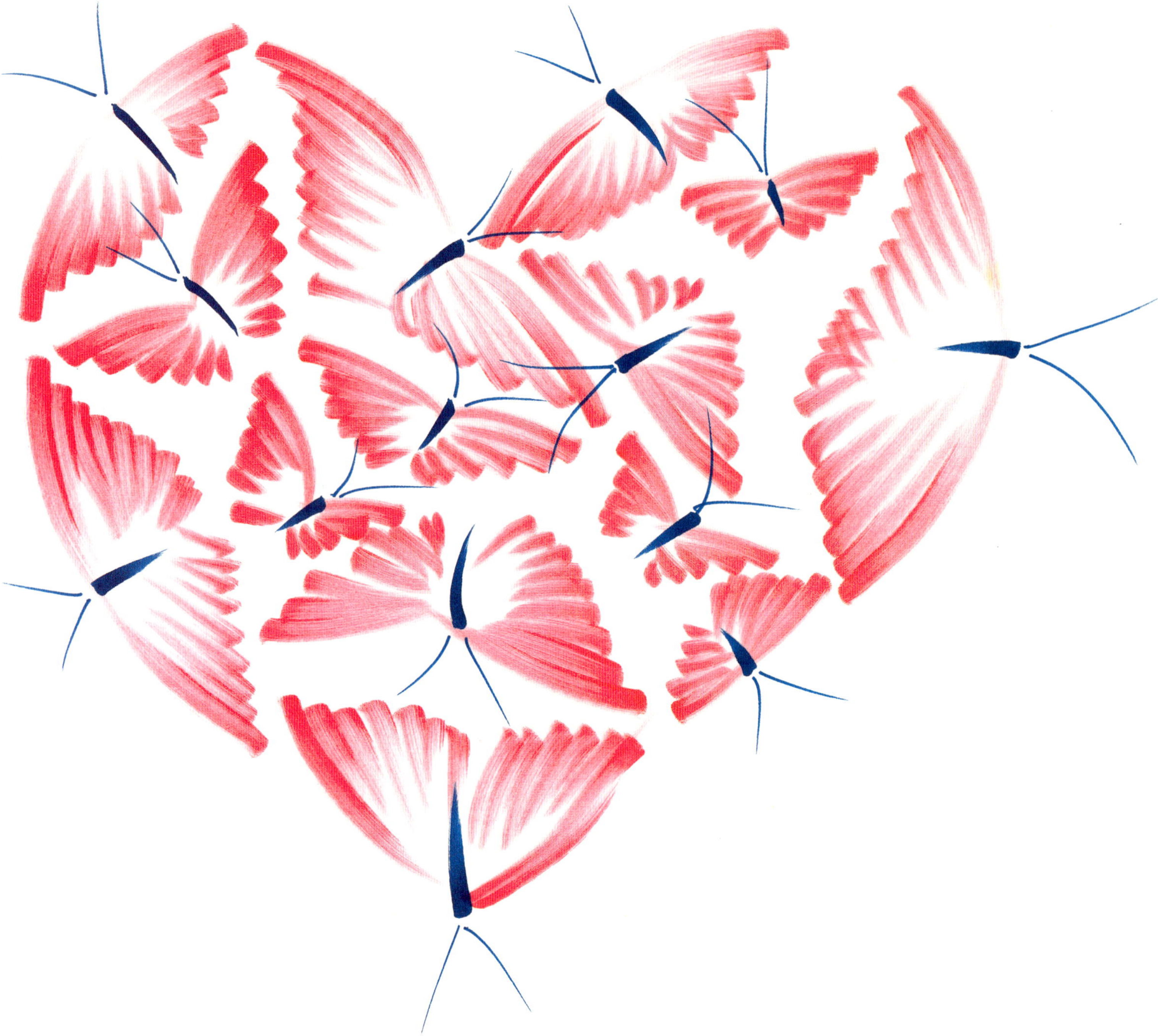

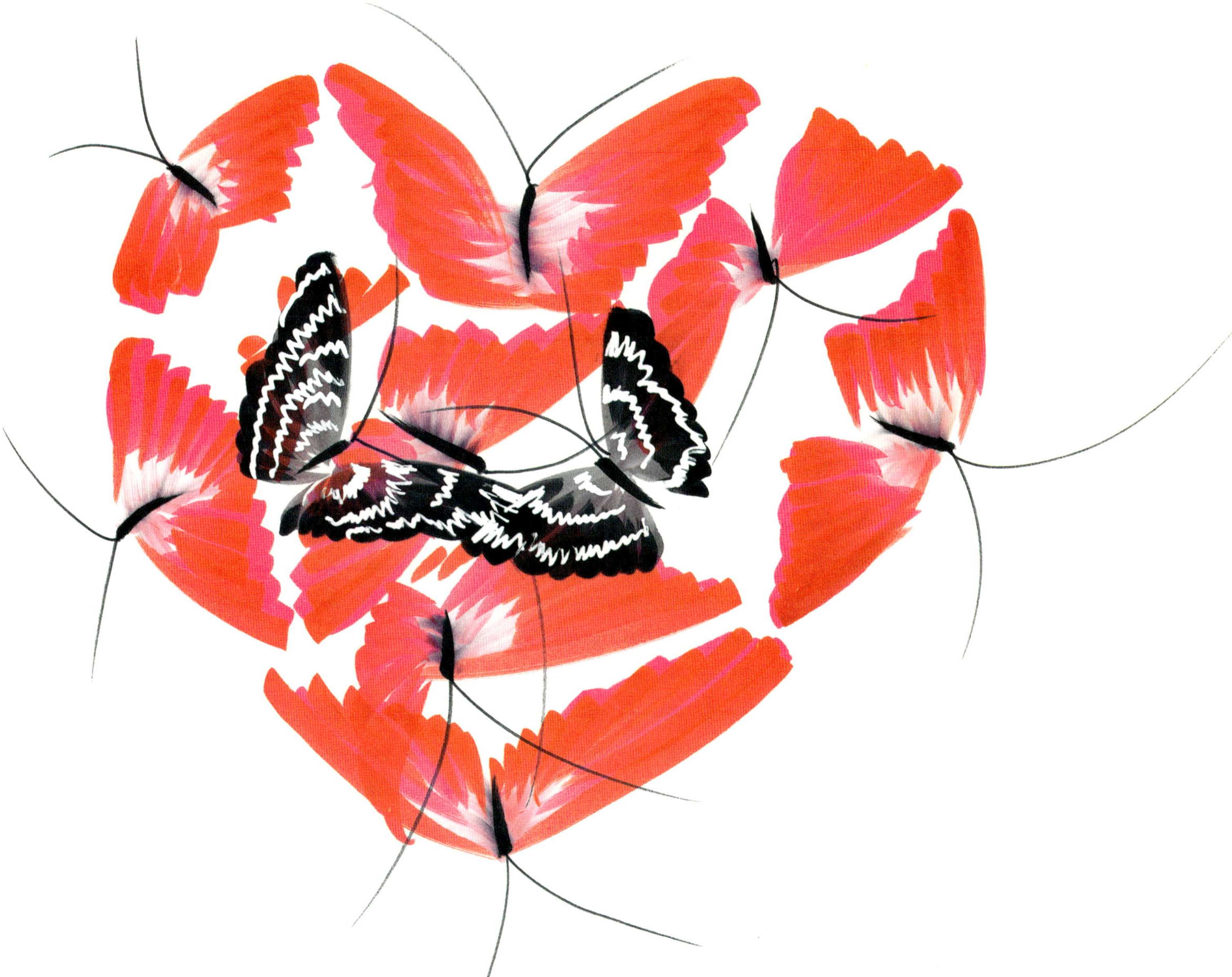

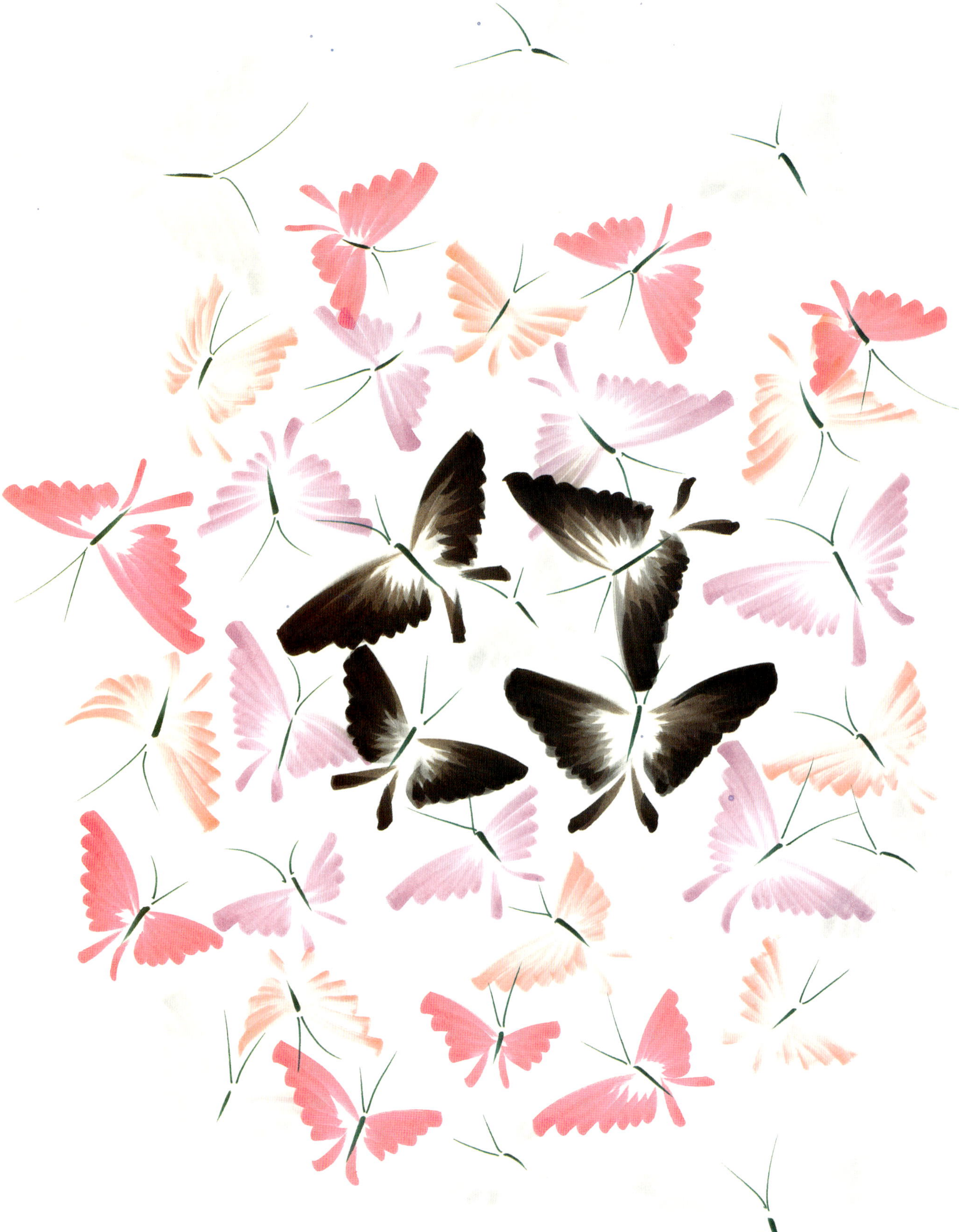

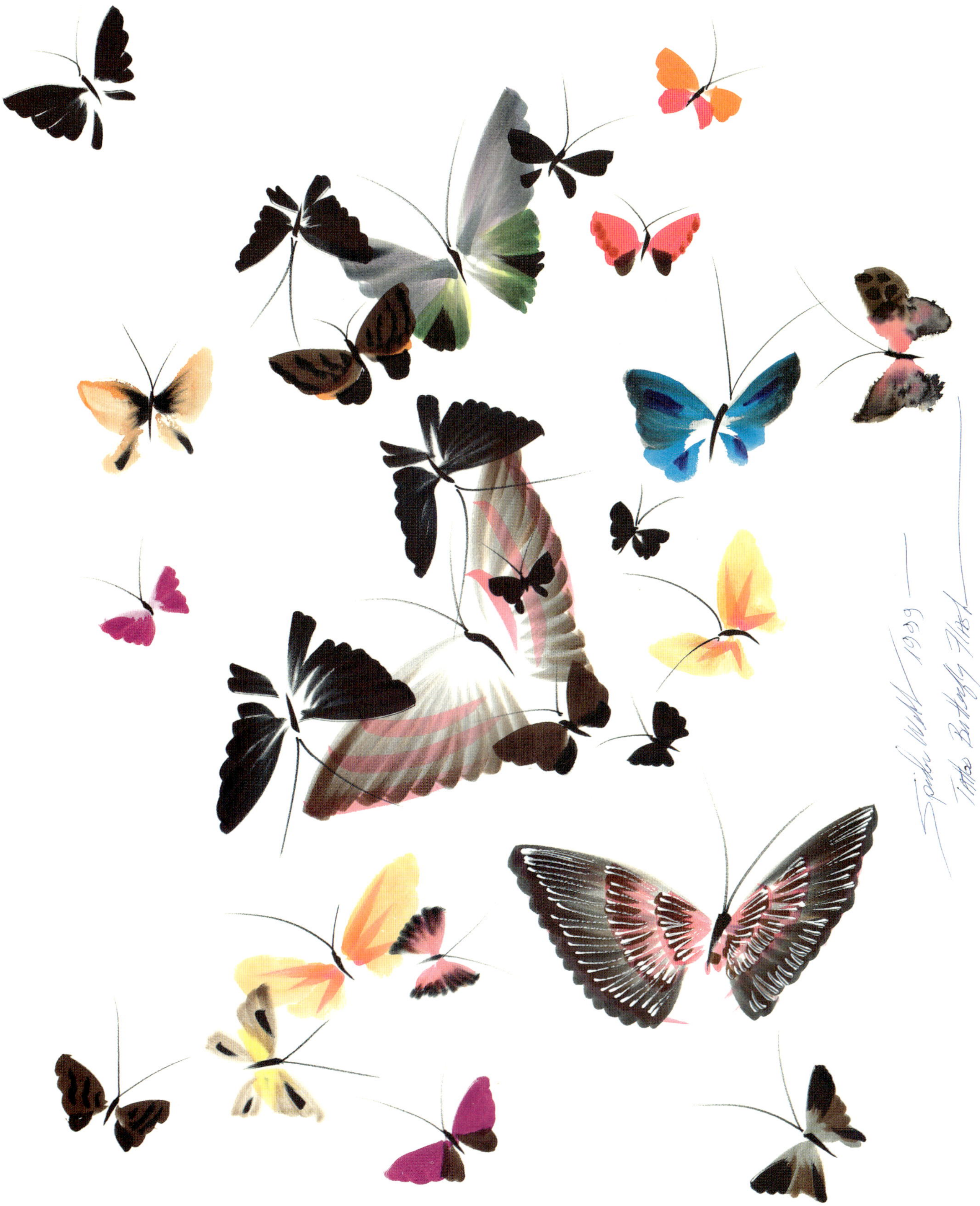
1999
Tattoo Butterfly Flash

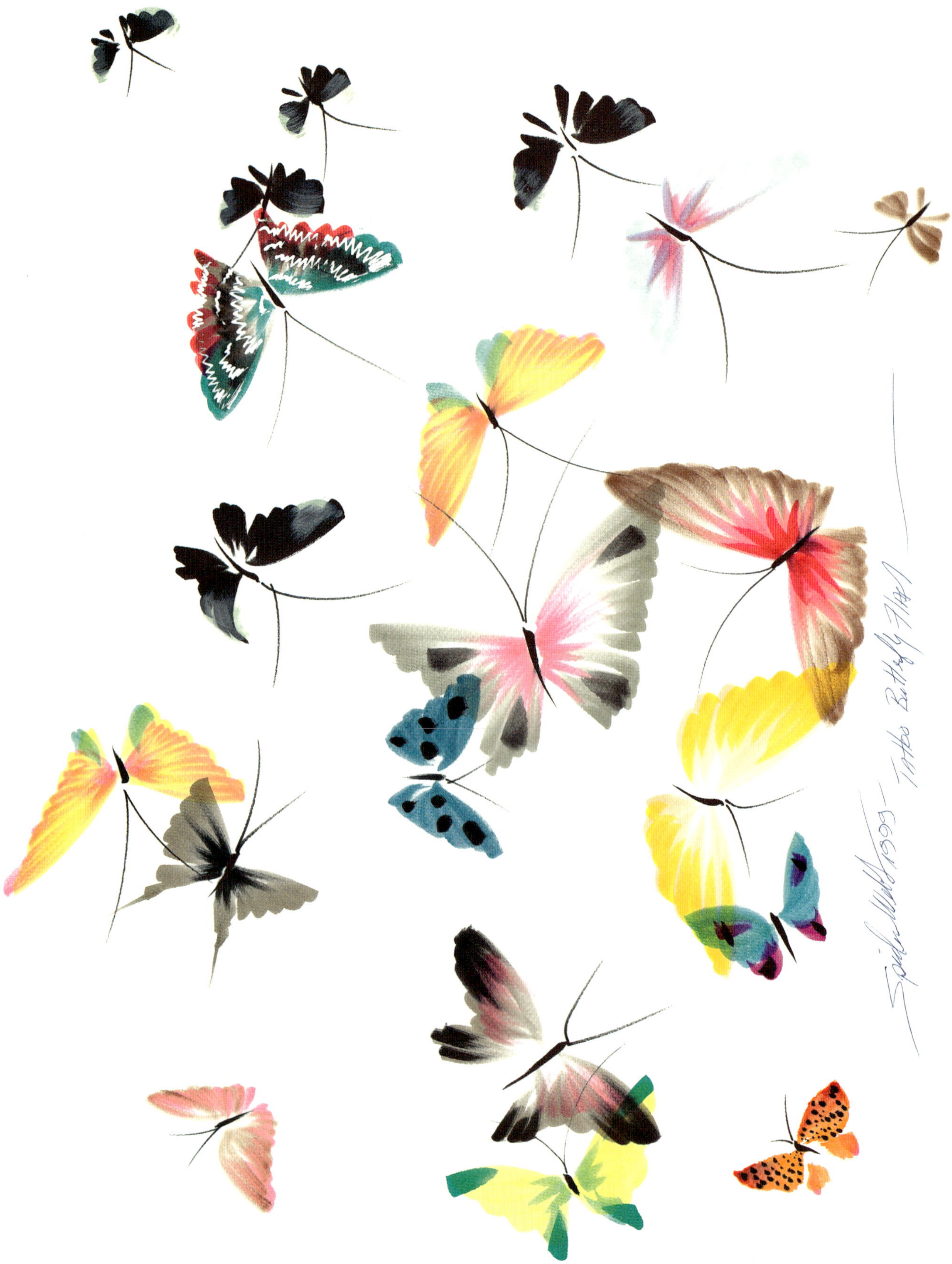
Tattoo Butterfly Flash

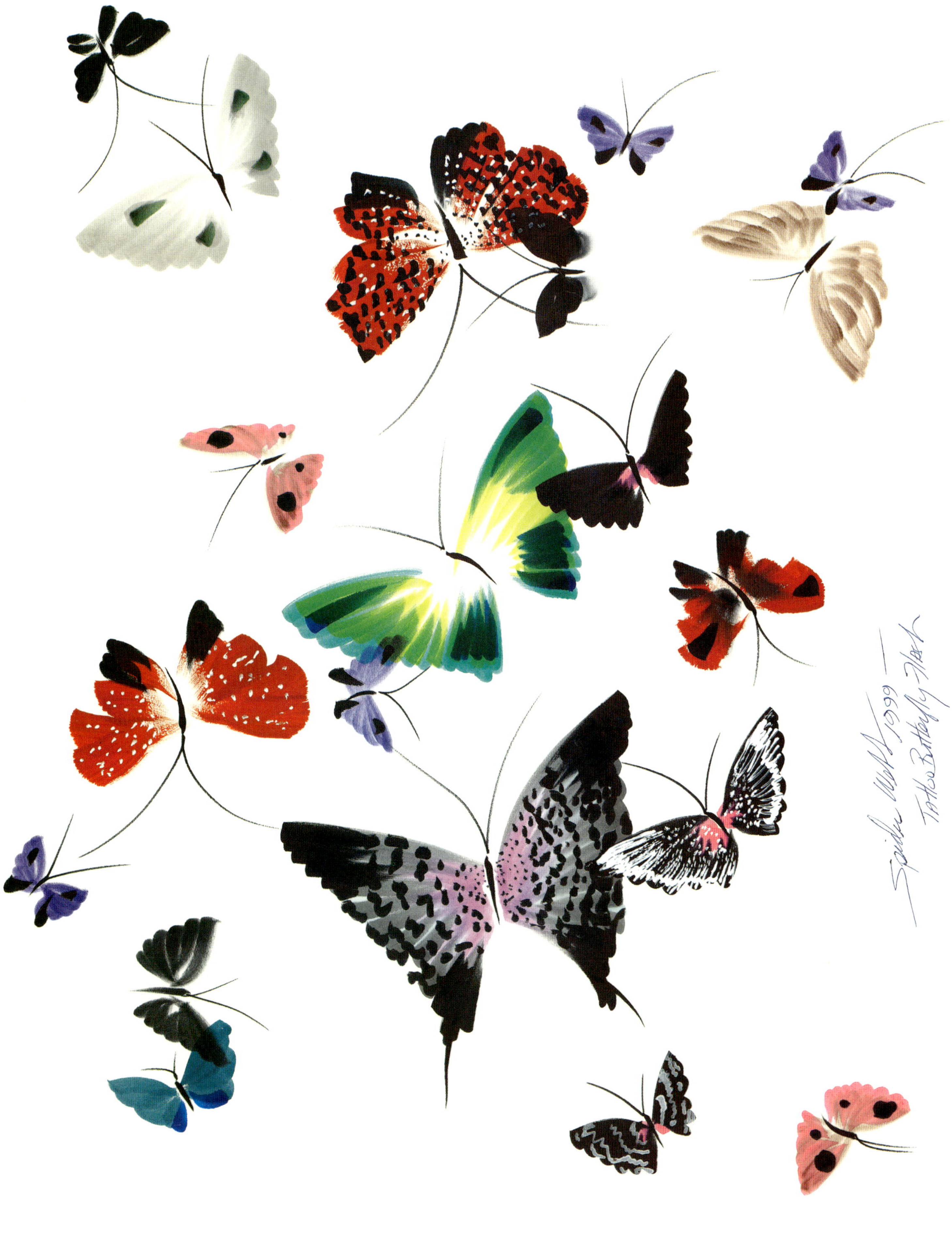

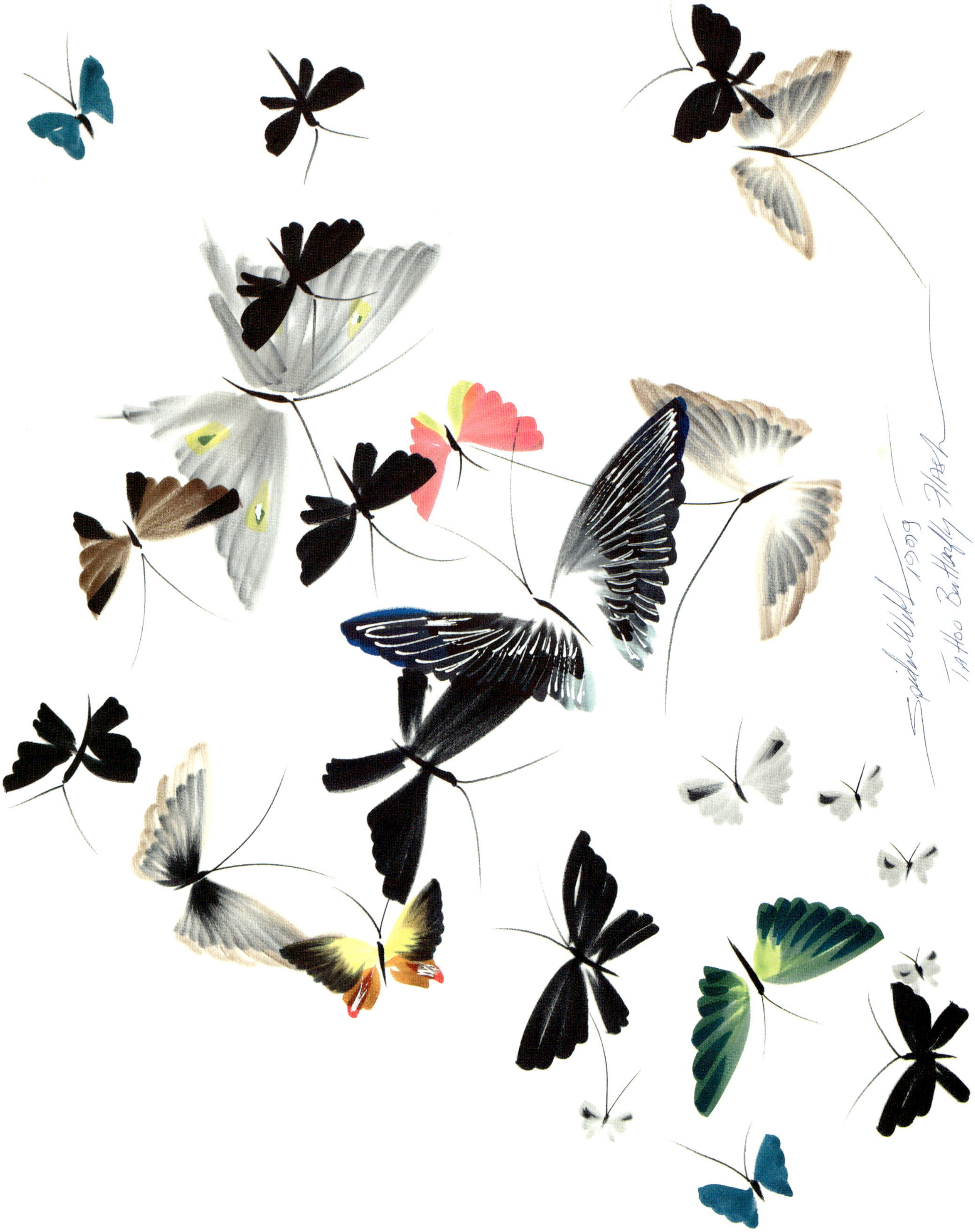
Tattoo Butterfly Flash

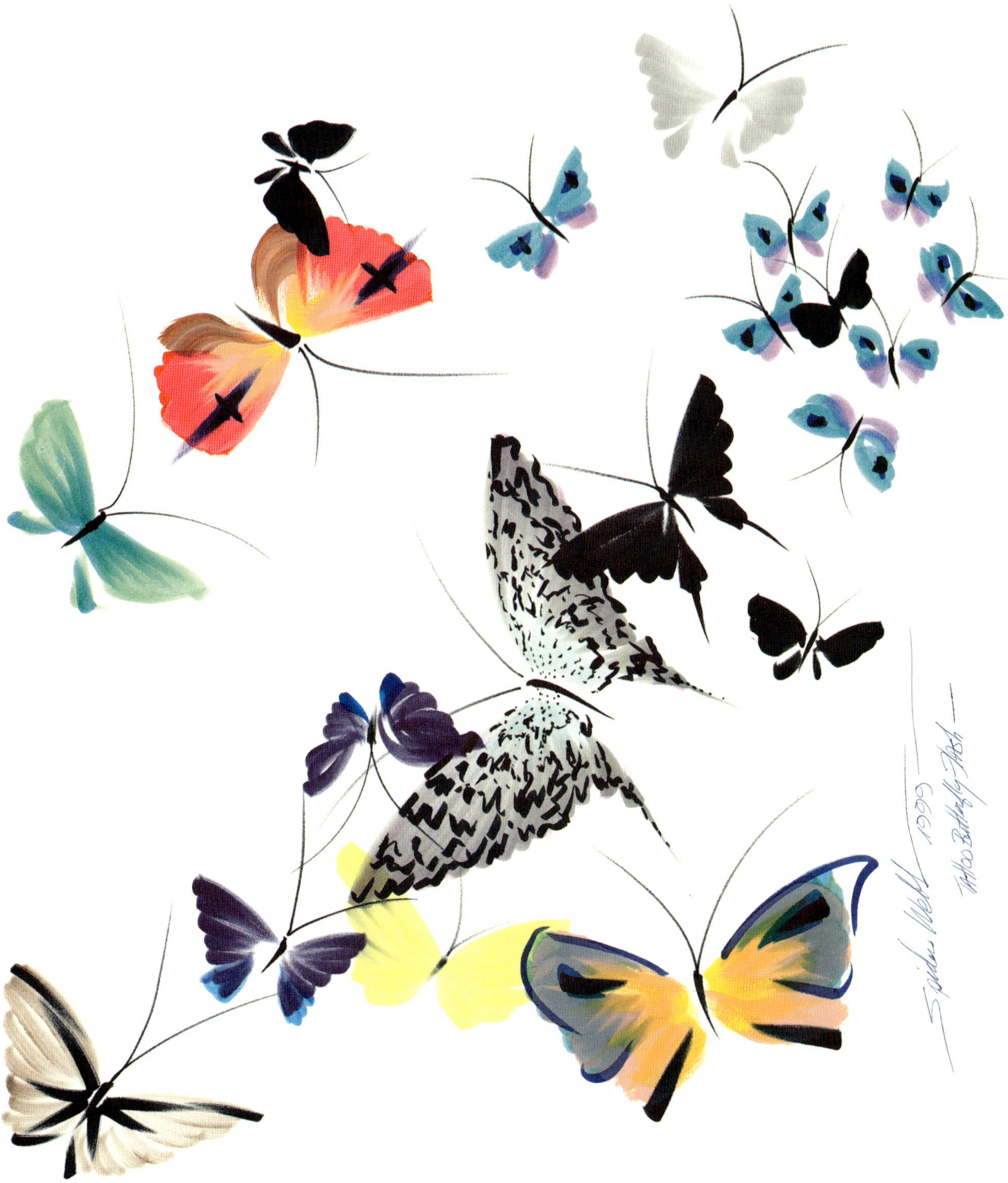

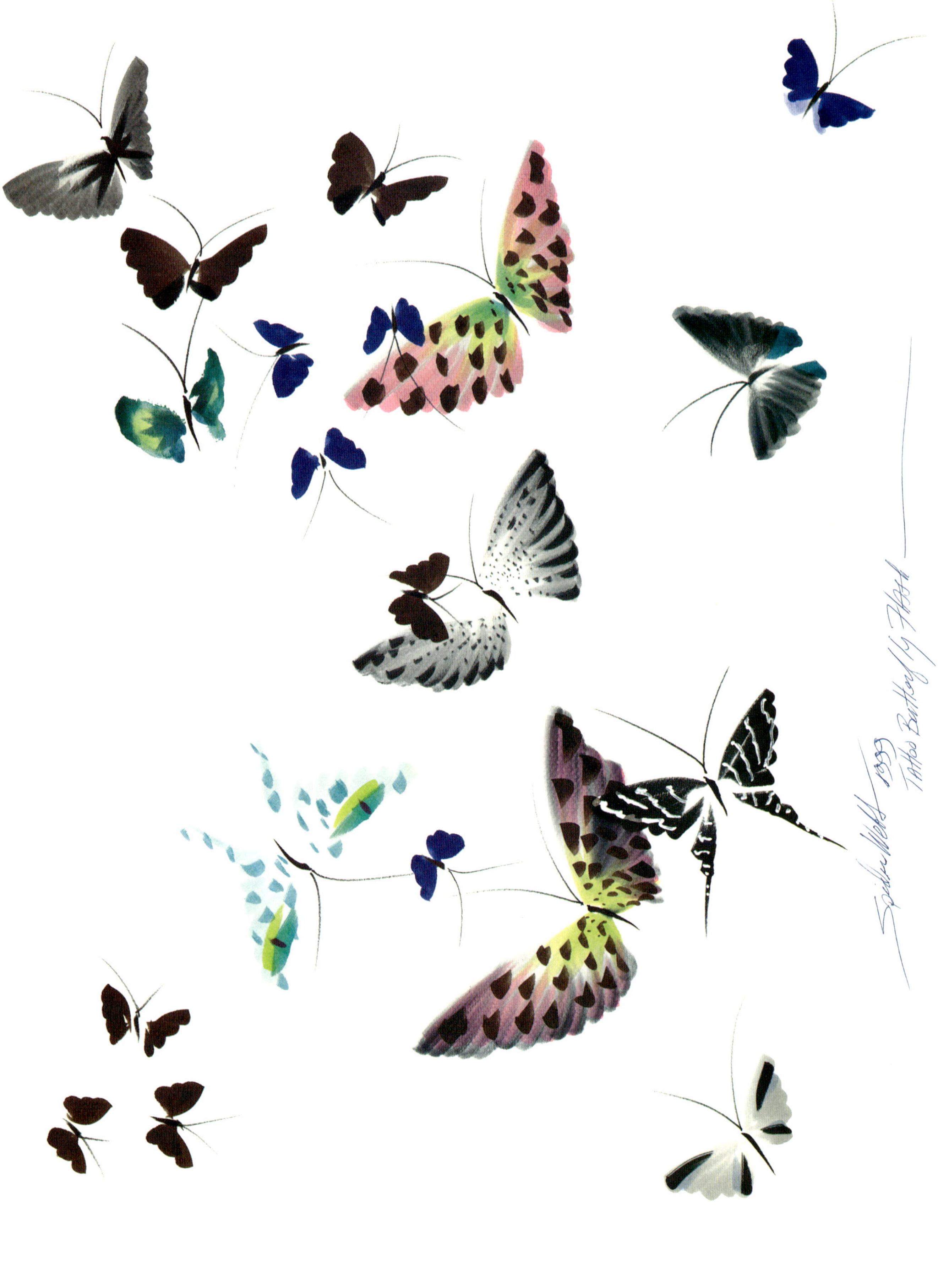
Spider Webb 1993
Tattoo Butterfly Flash

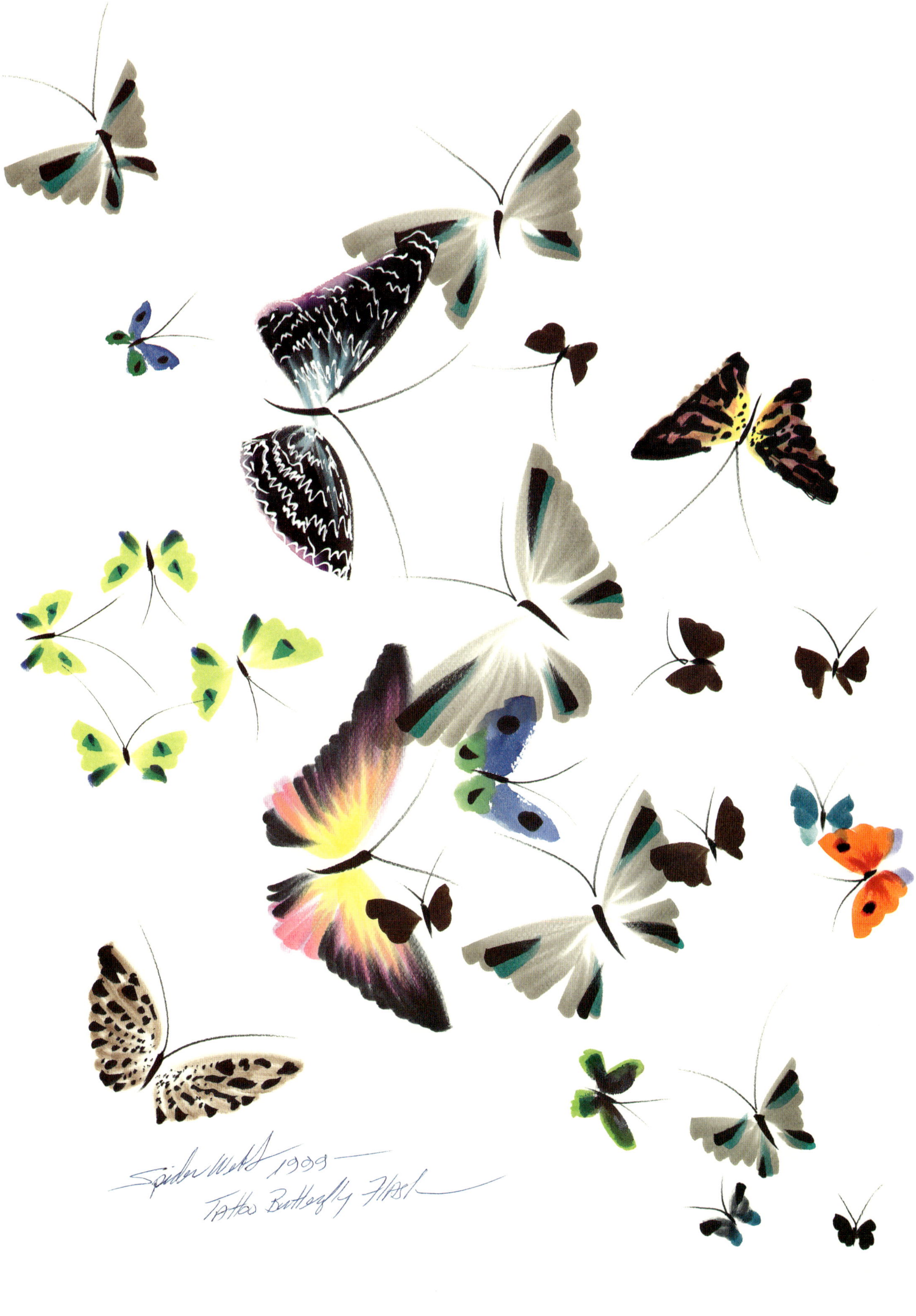
Spider Webb 1999
Tattoo Butterfly Flash

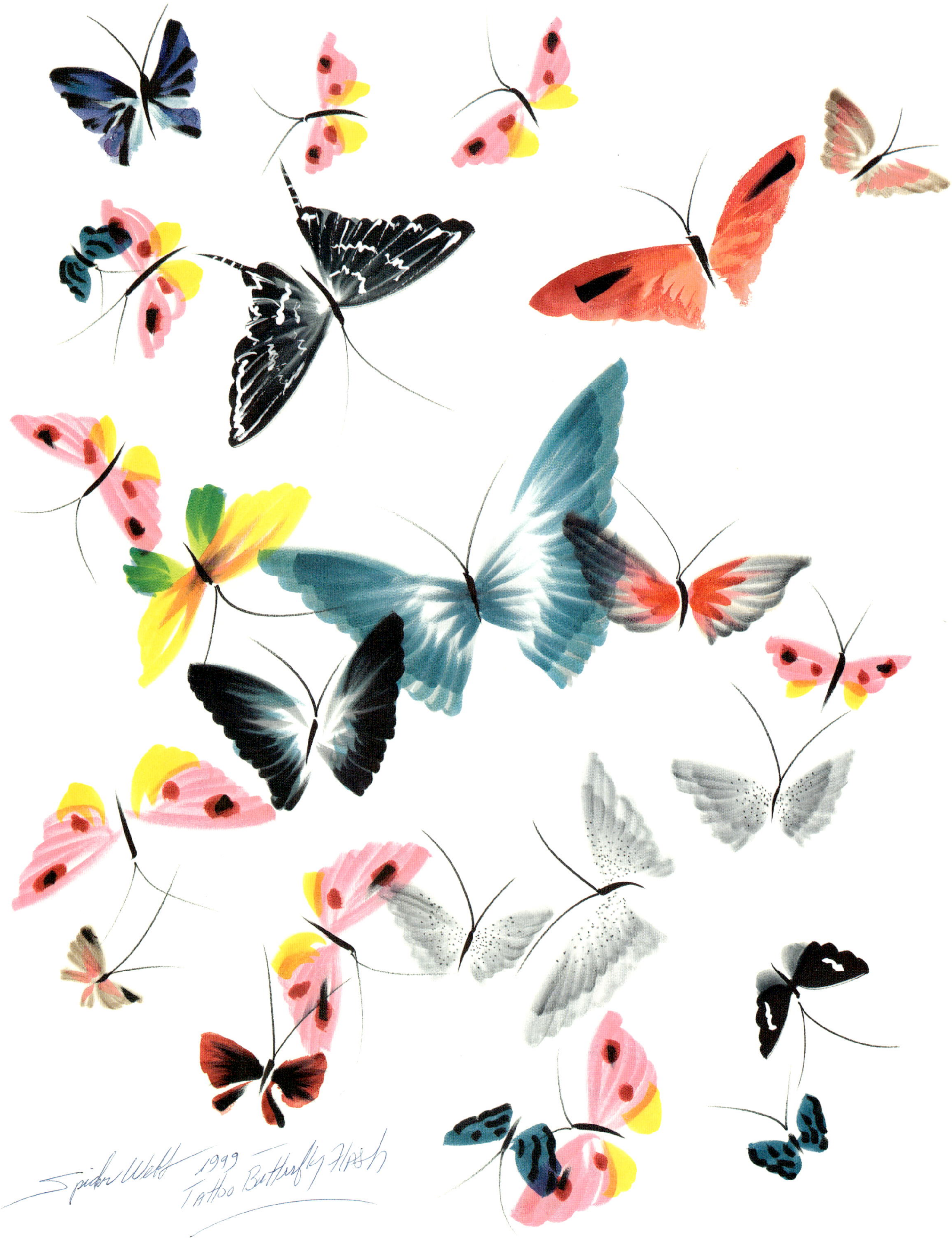
Spider Webb
1999
Tattoo Butterfly Flash

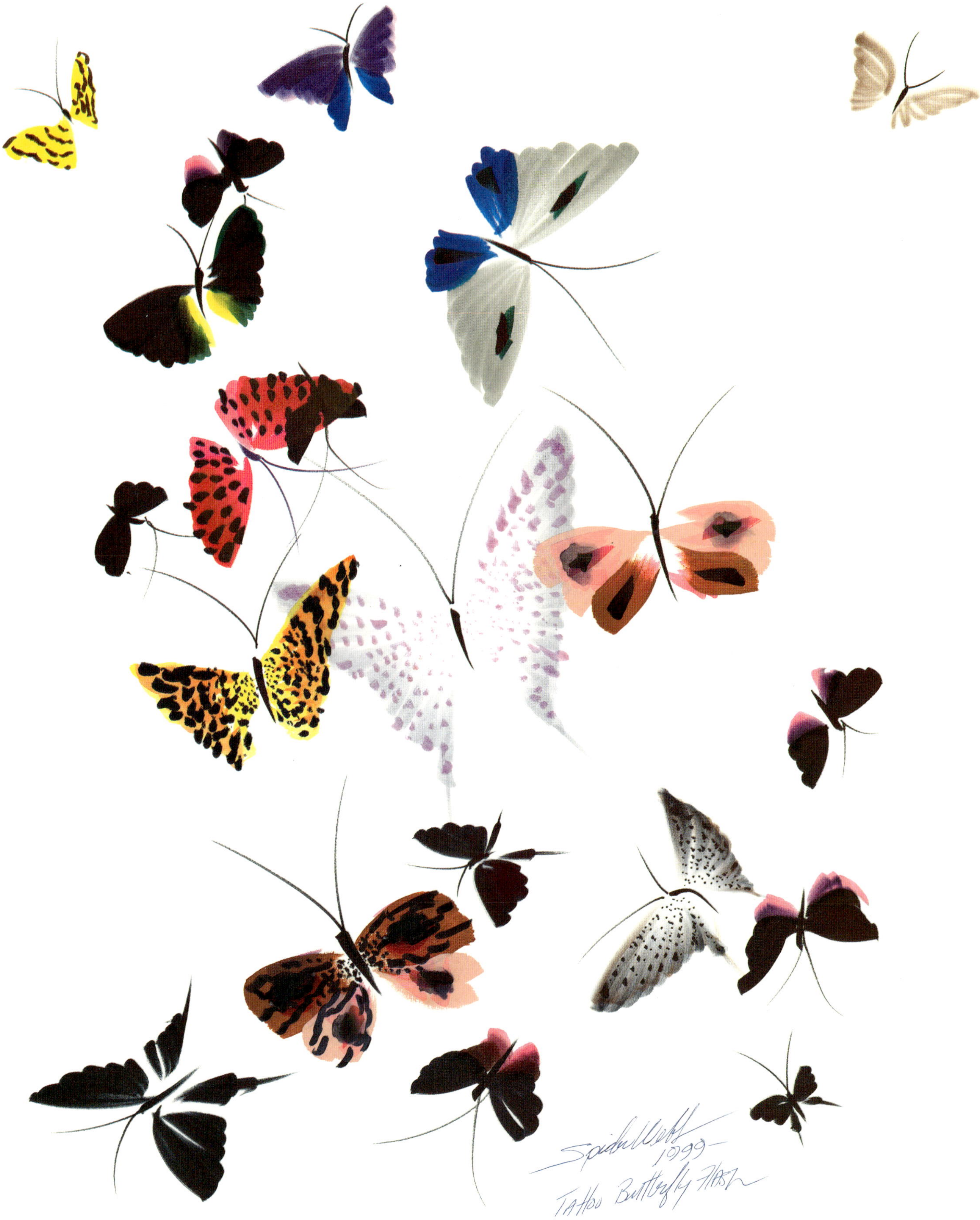
1999
Tattoo Butterfly Flash

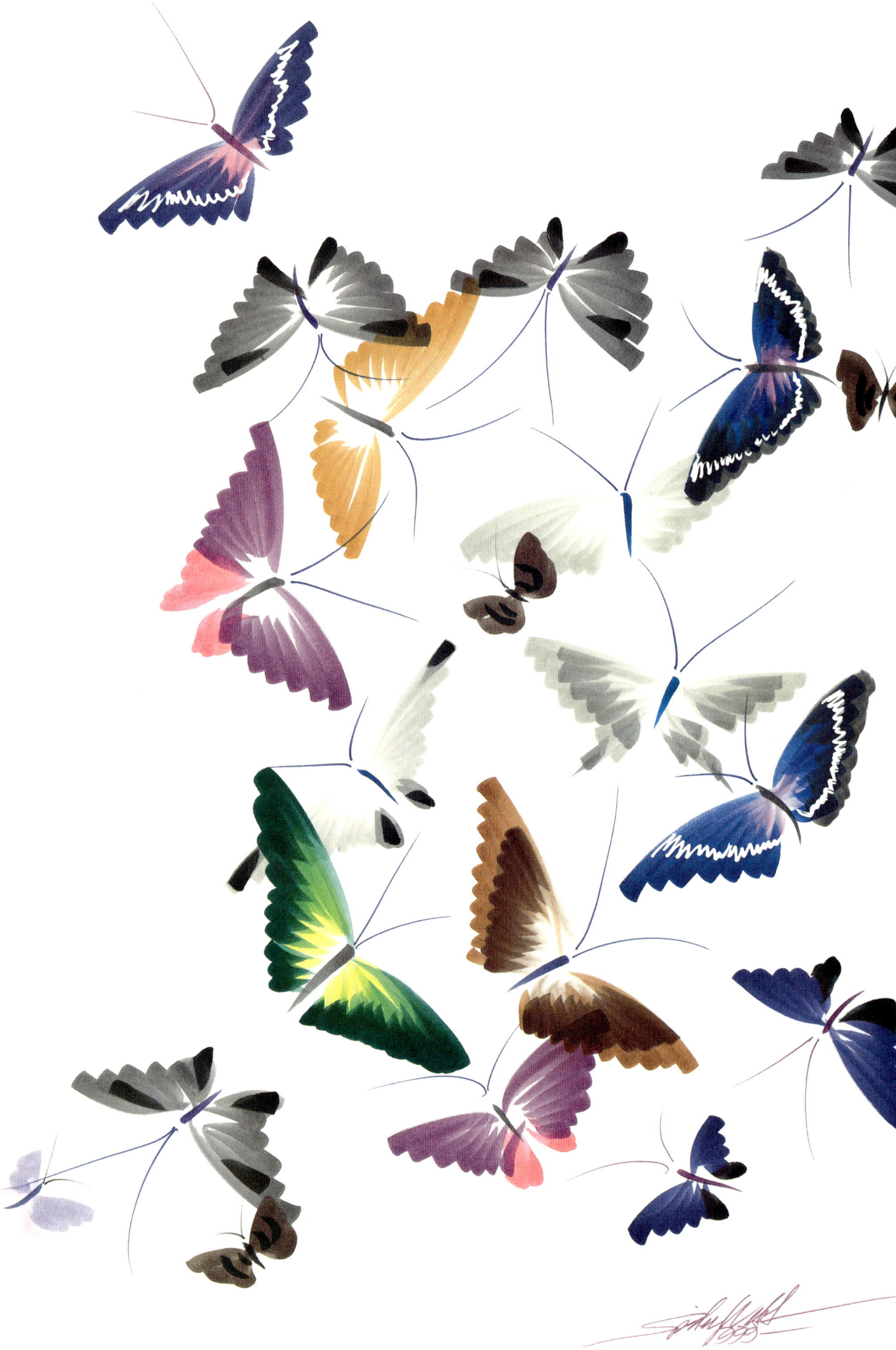

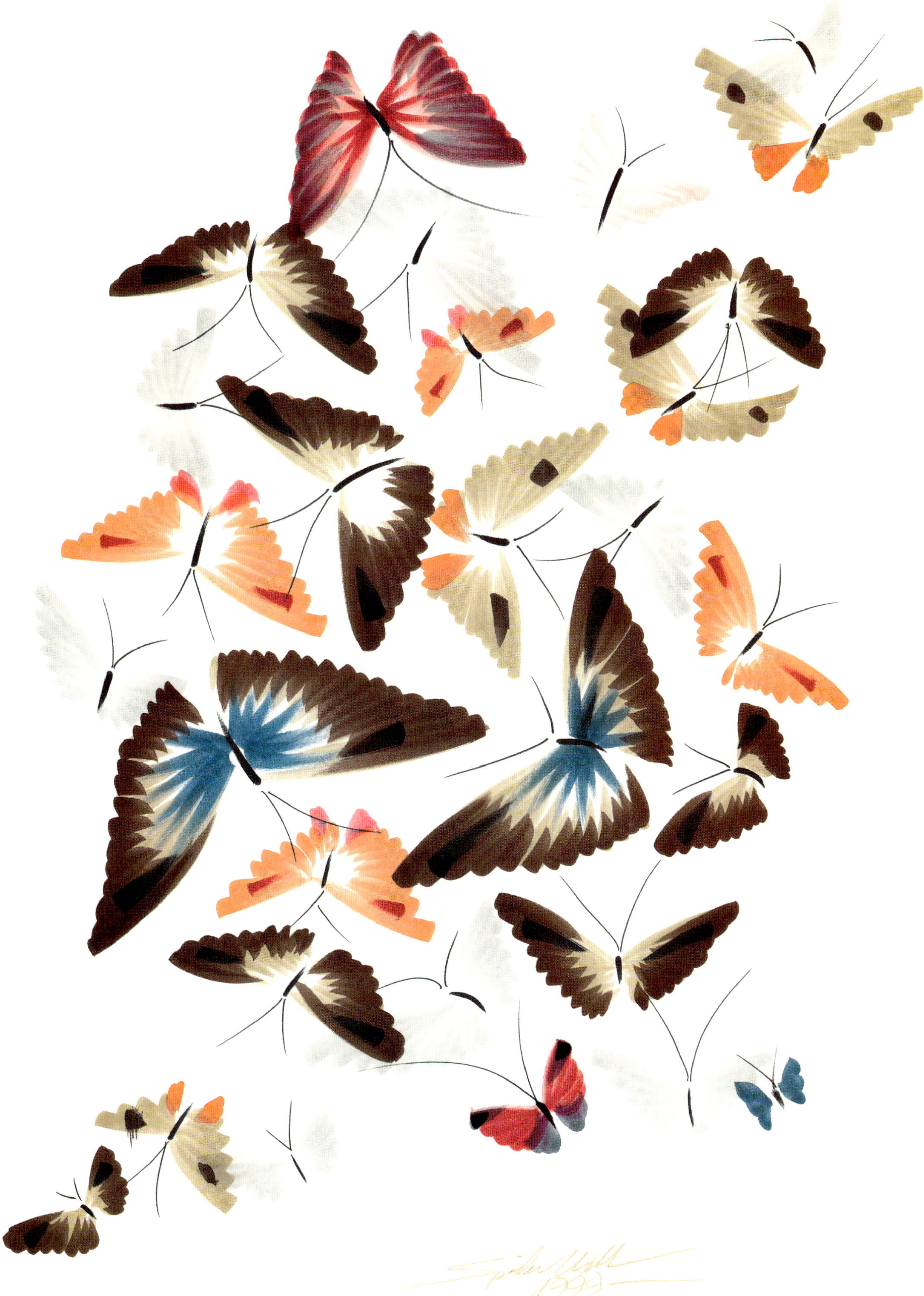

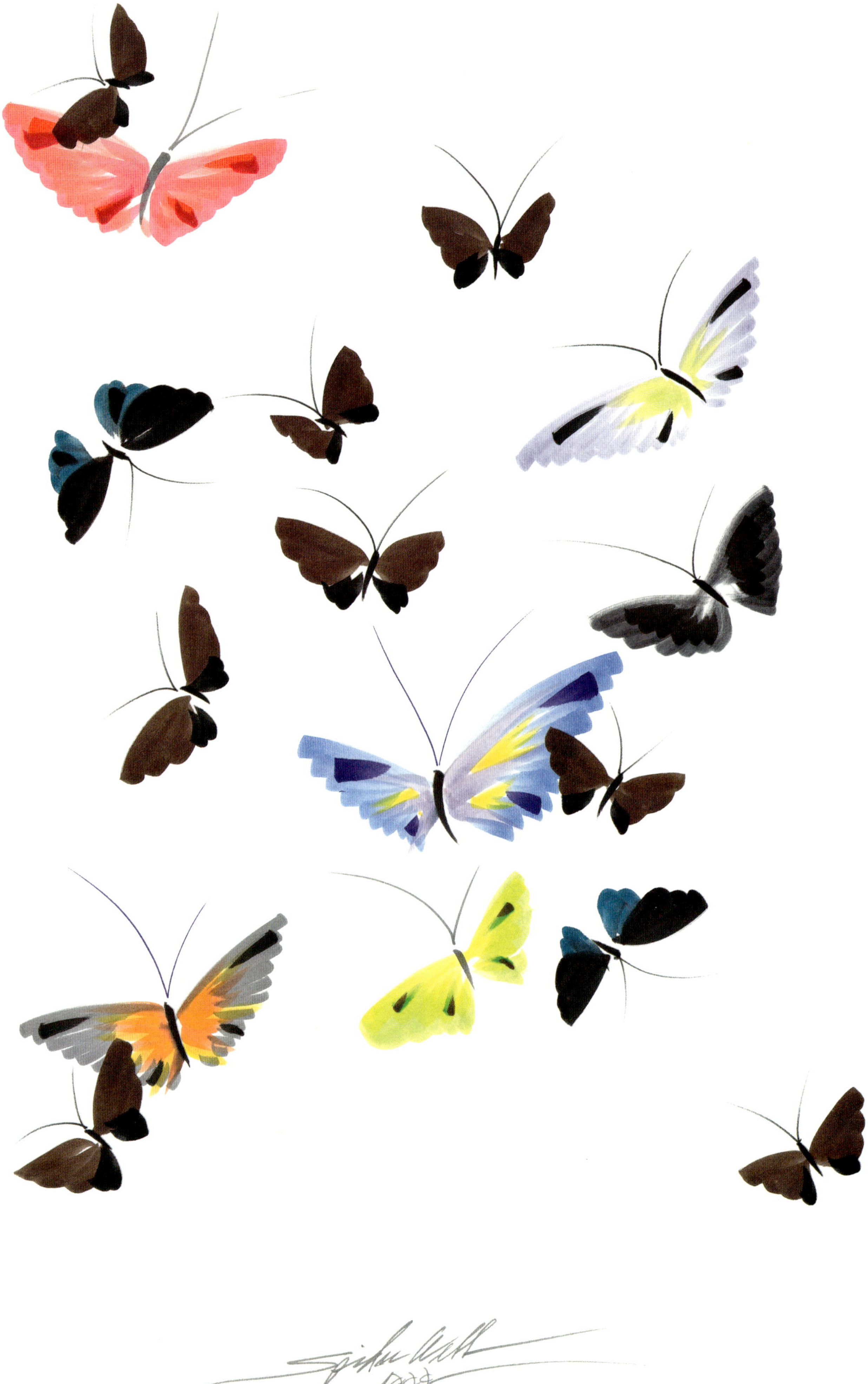

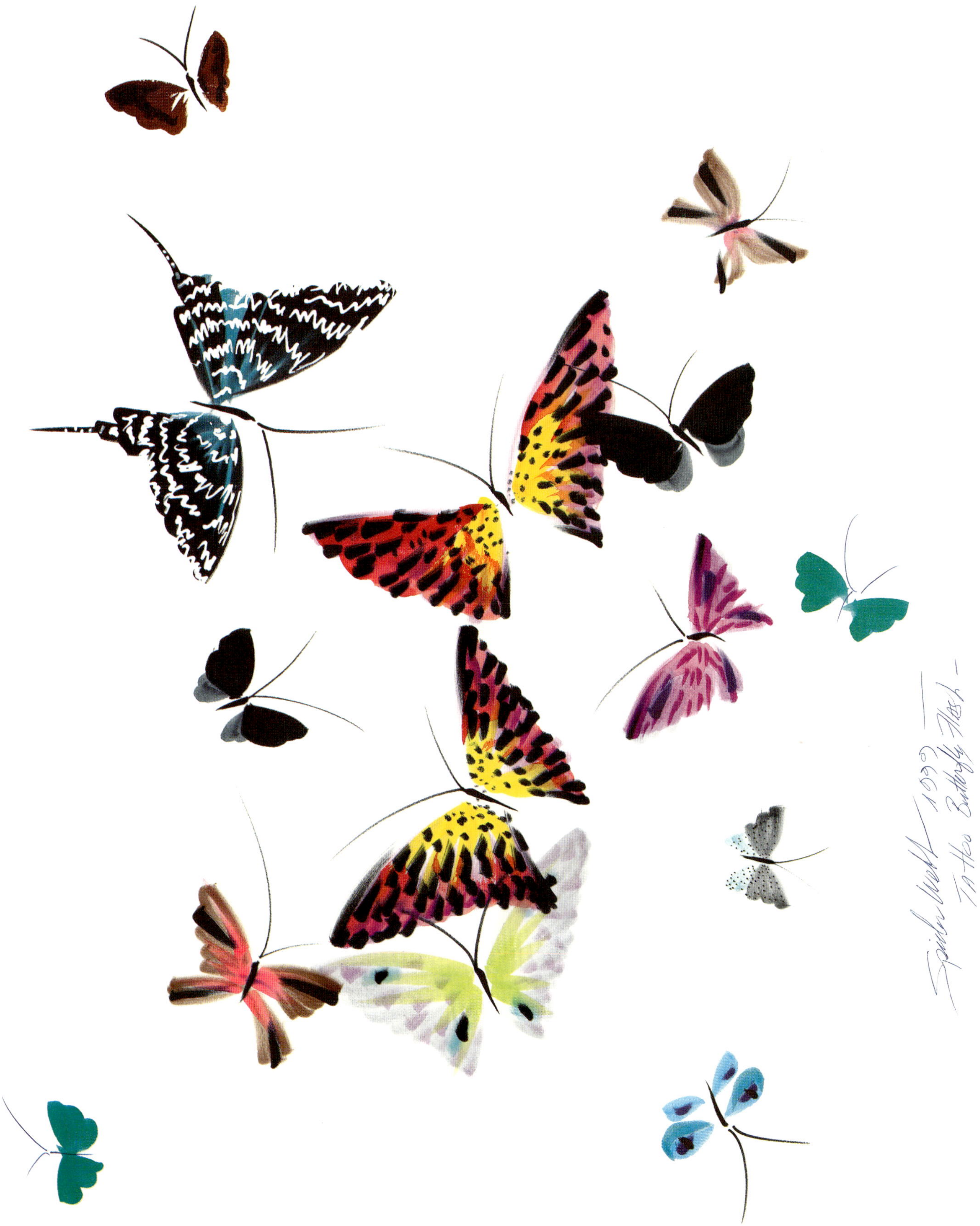
1993
Tattoo Butterfly Flash

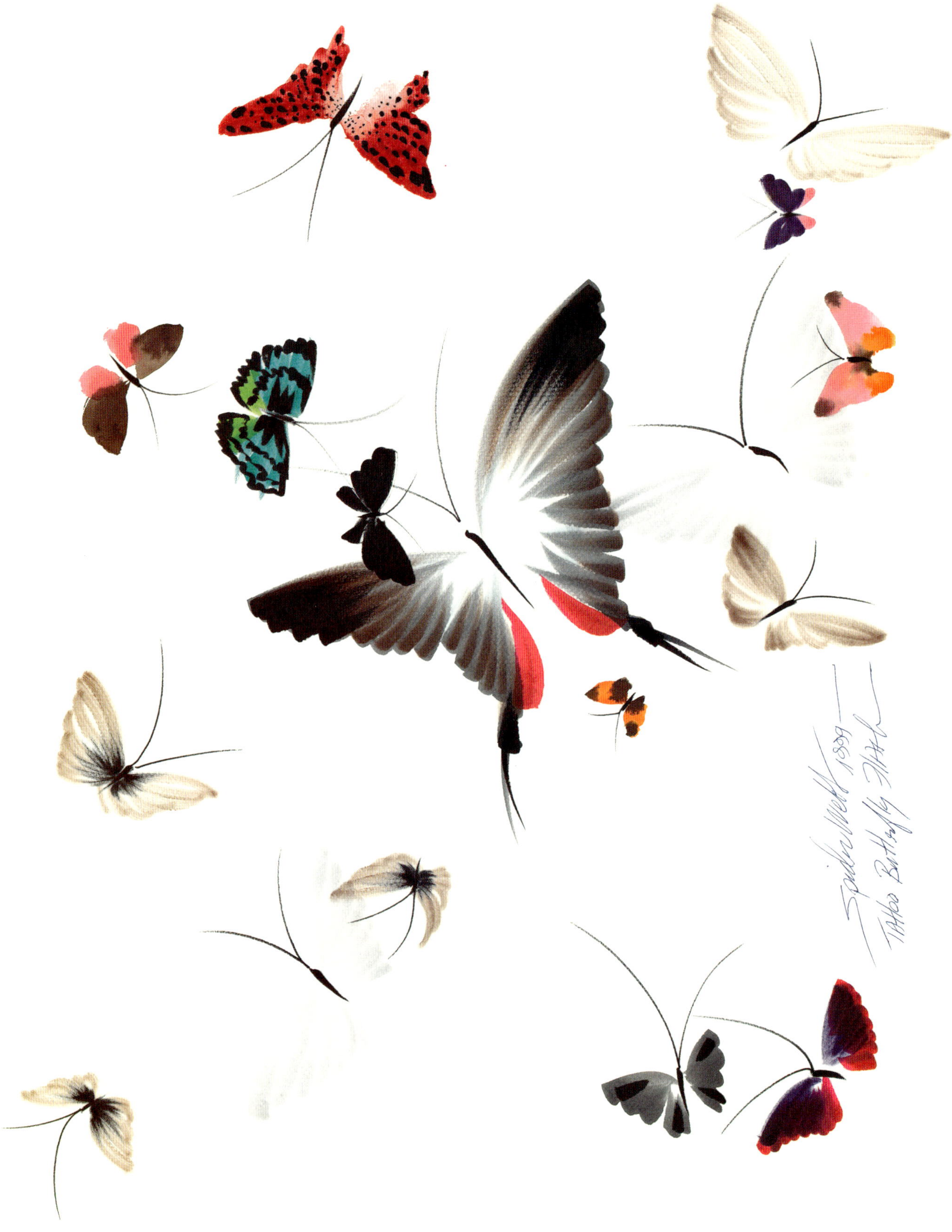

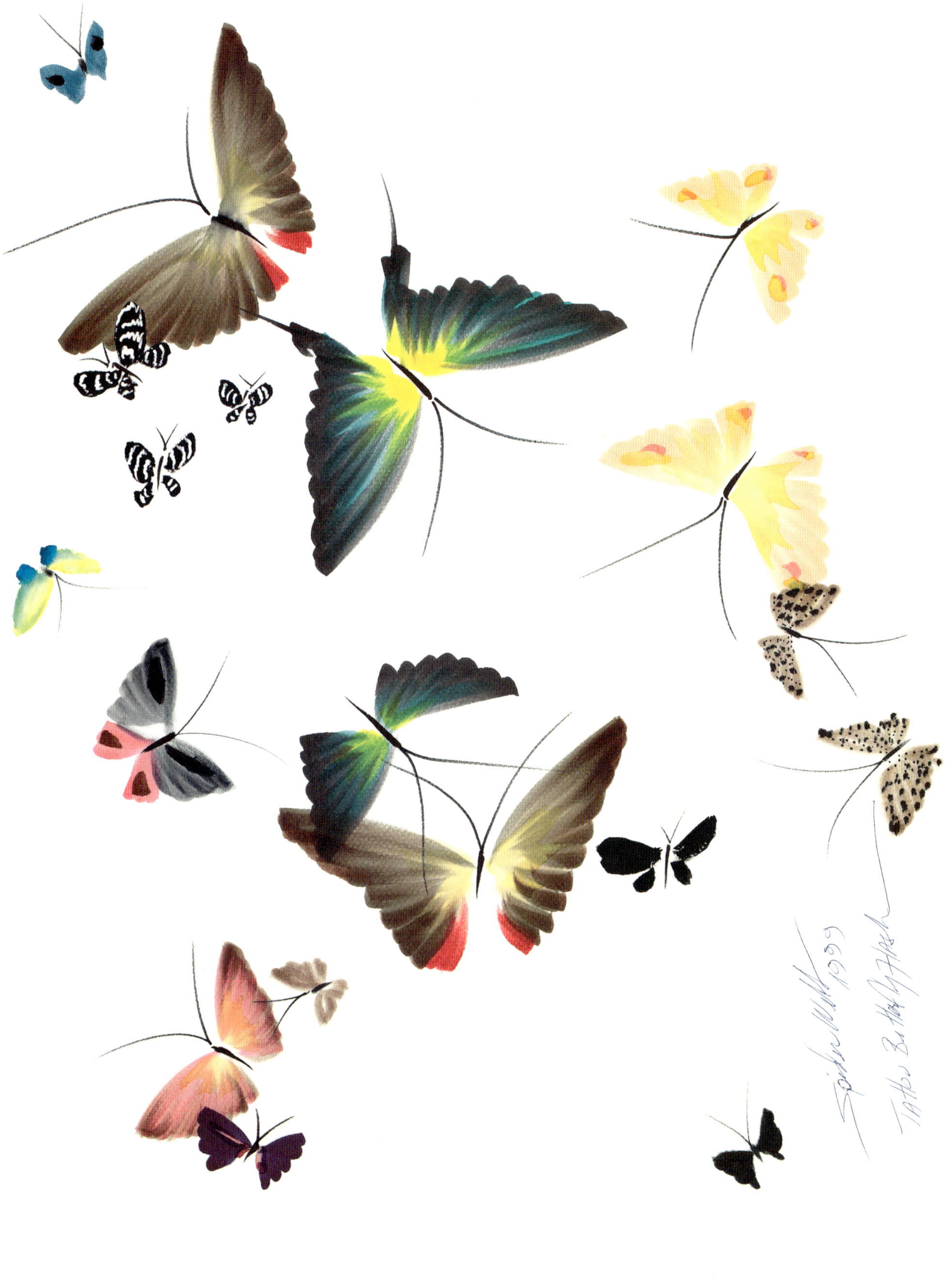

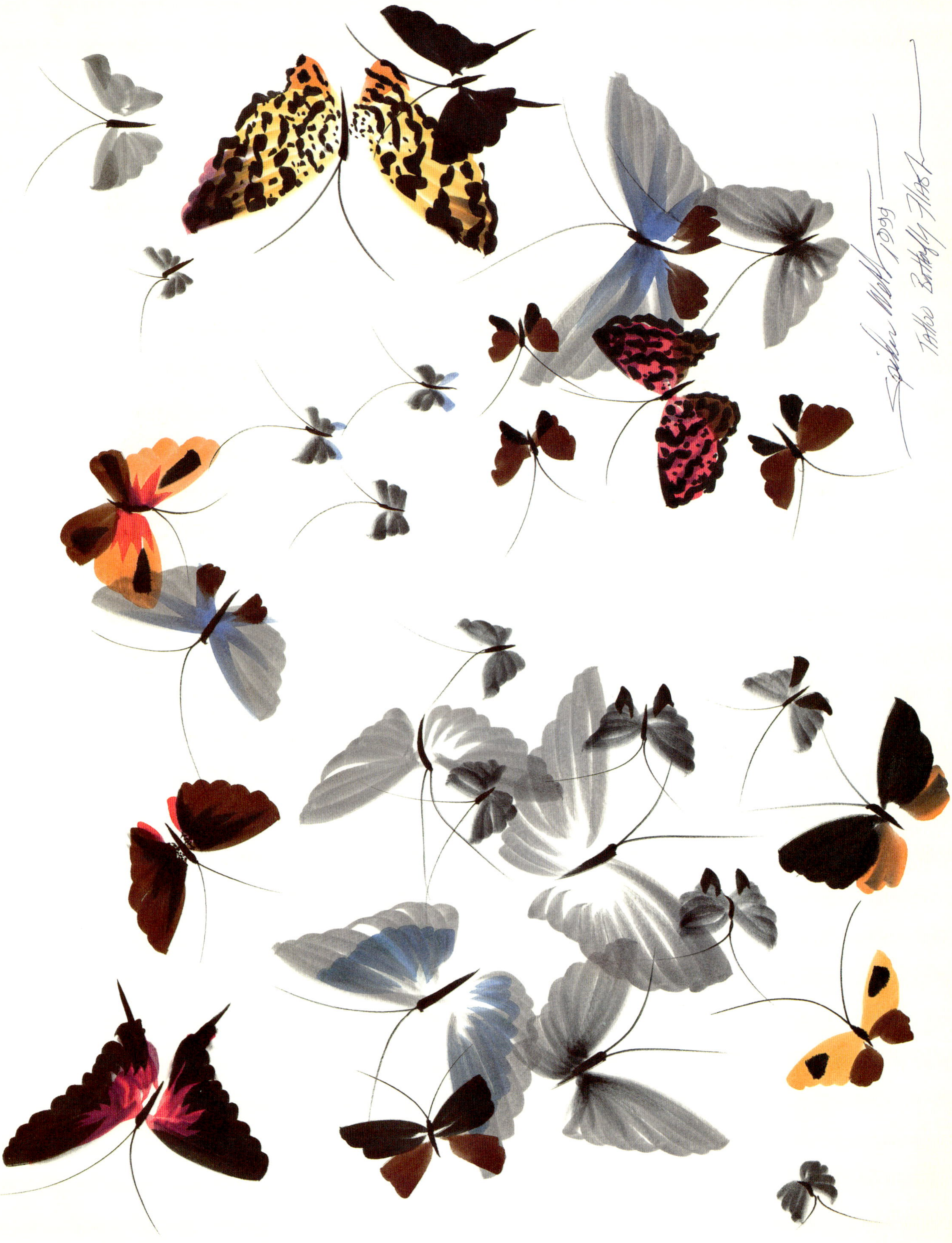

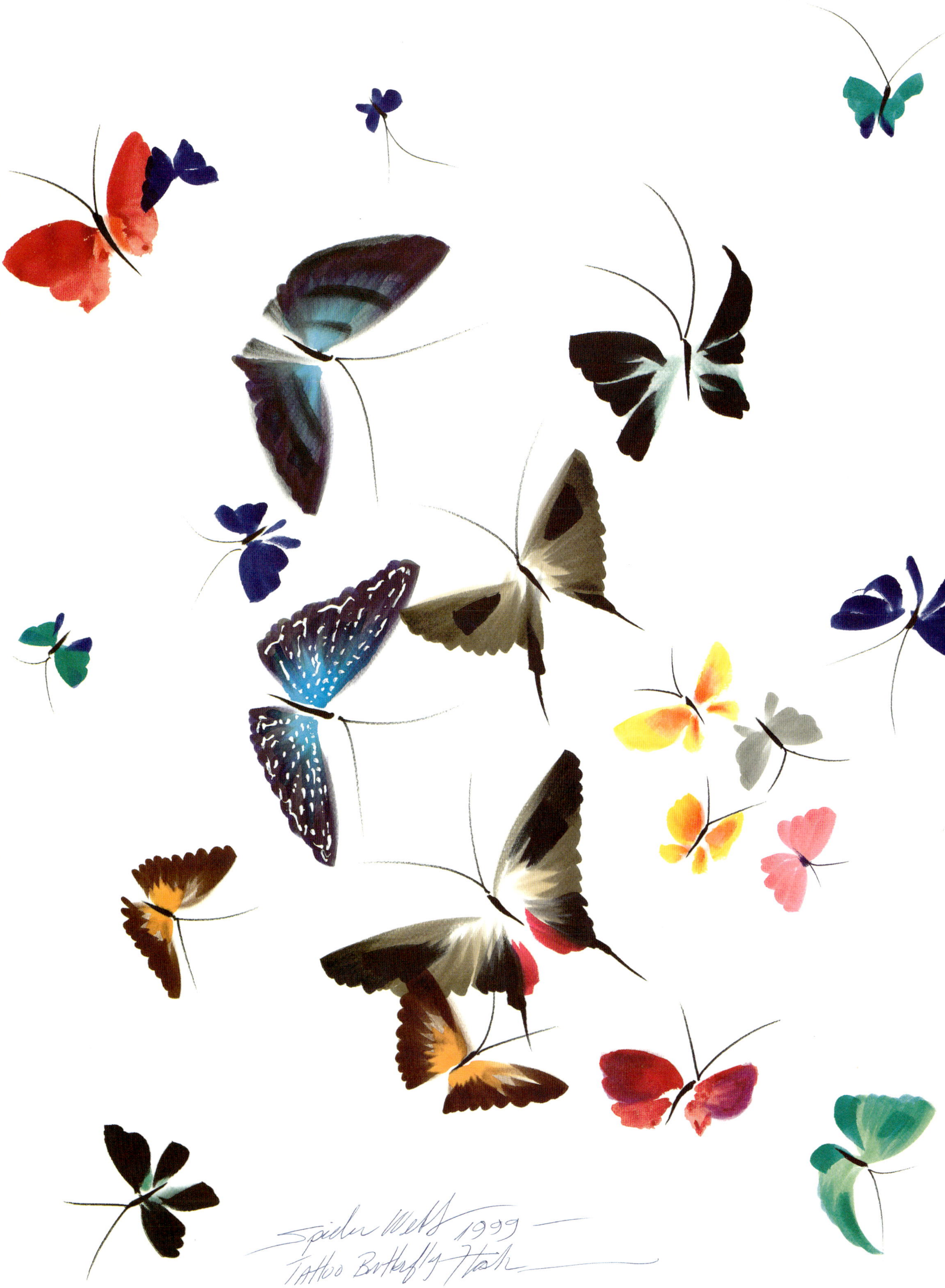
Spider Webb 1999
Tattoo Butterfly Flash

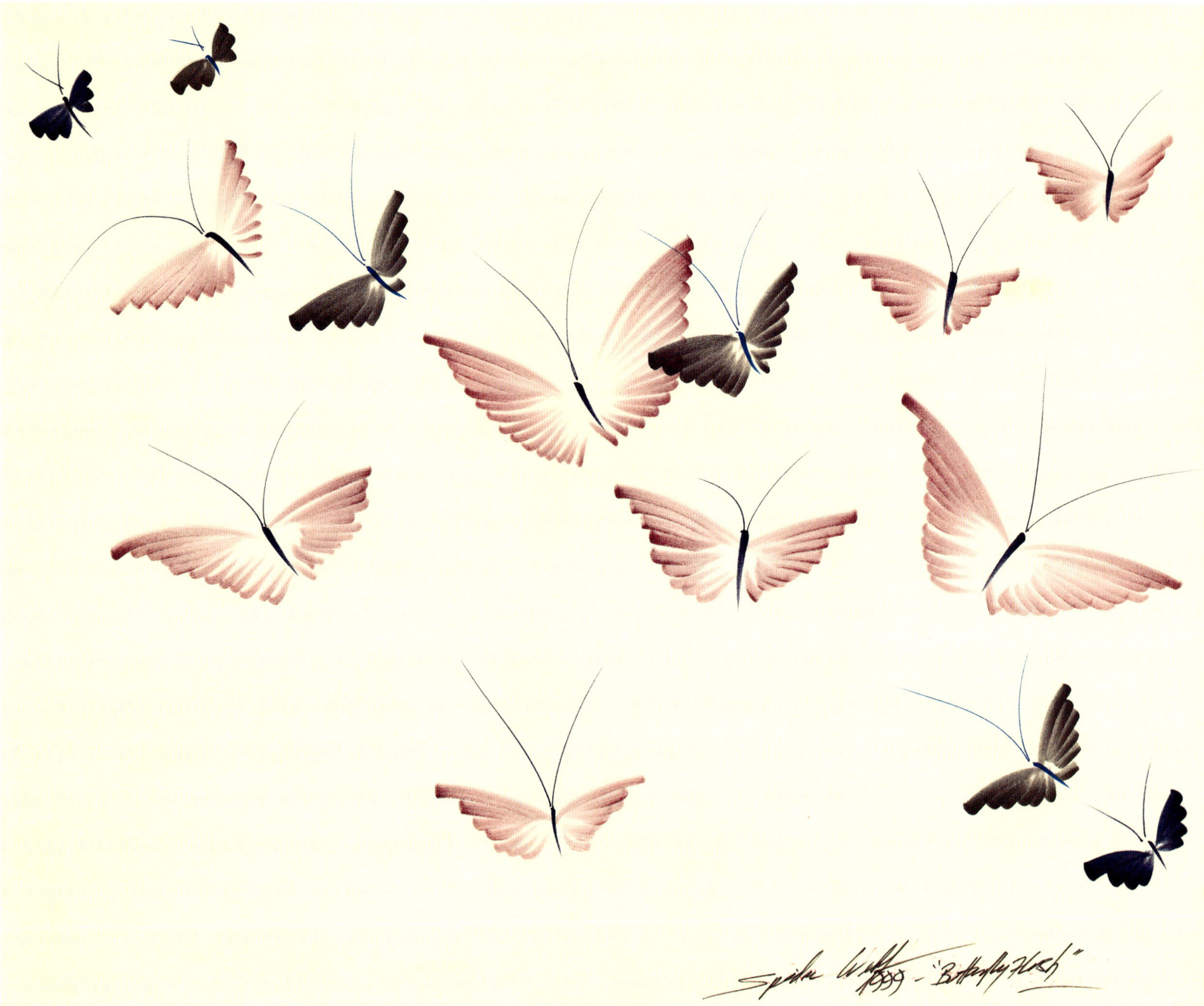

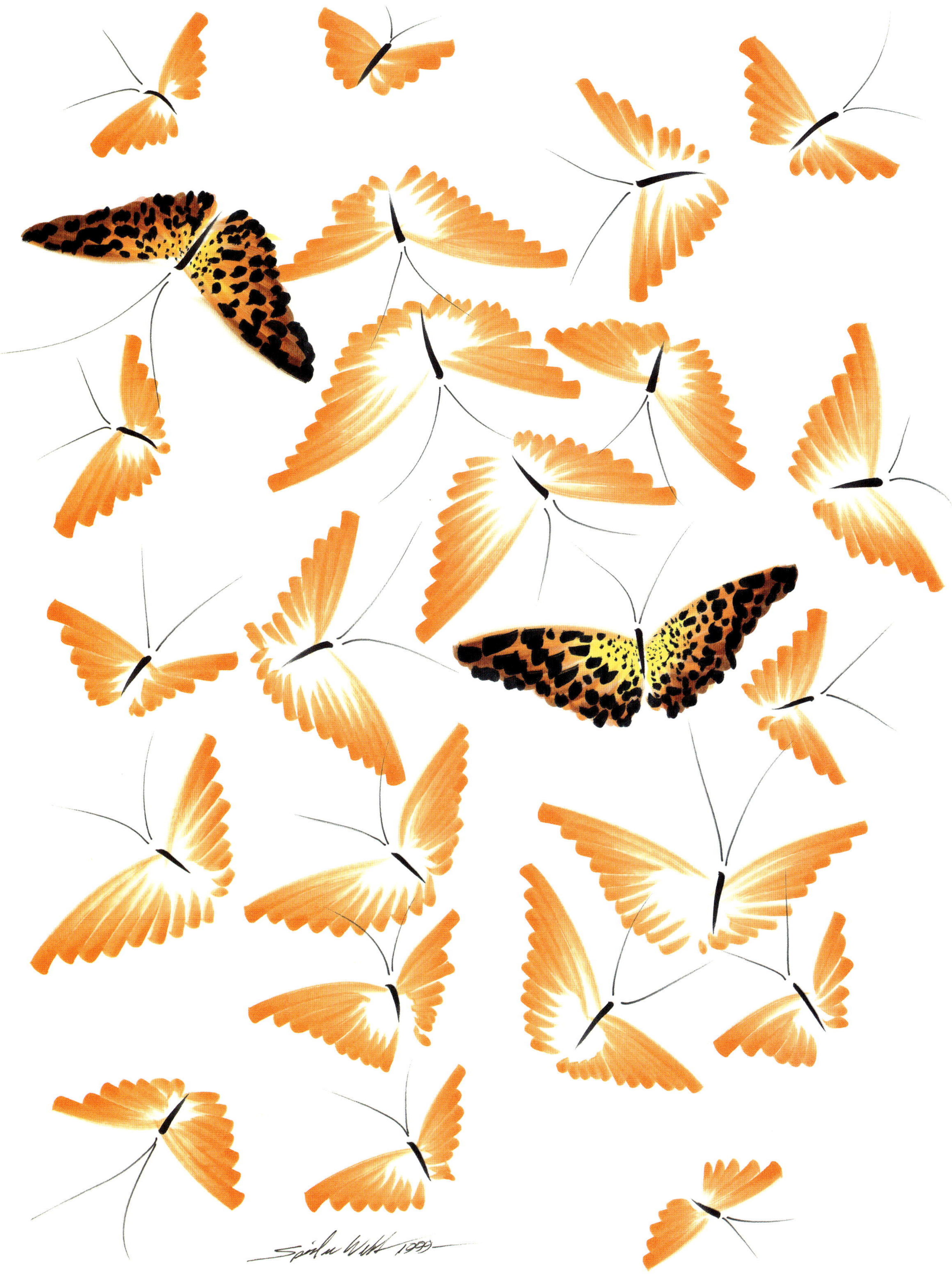

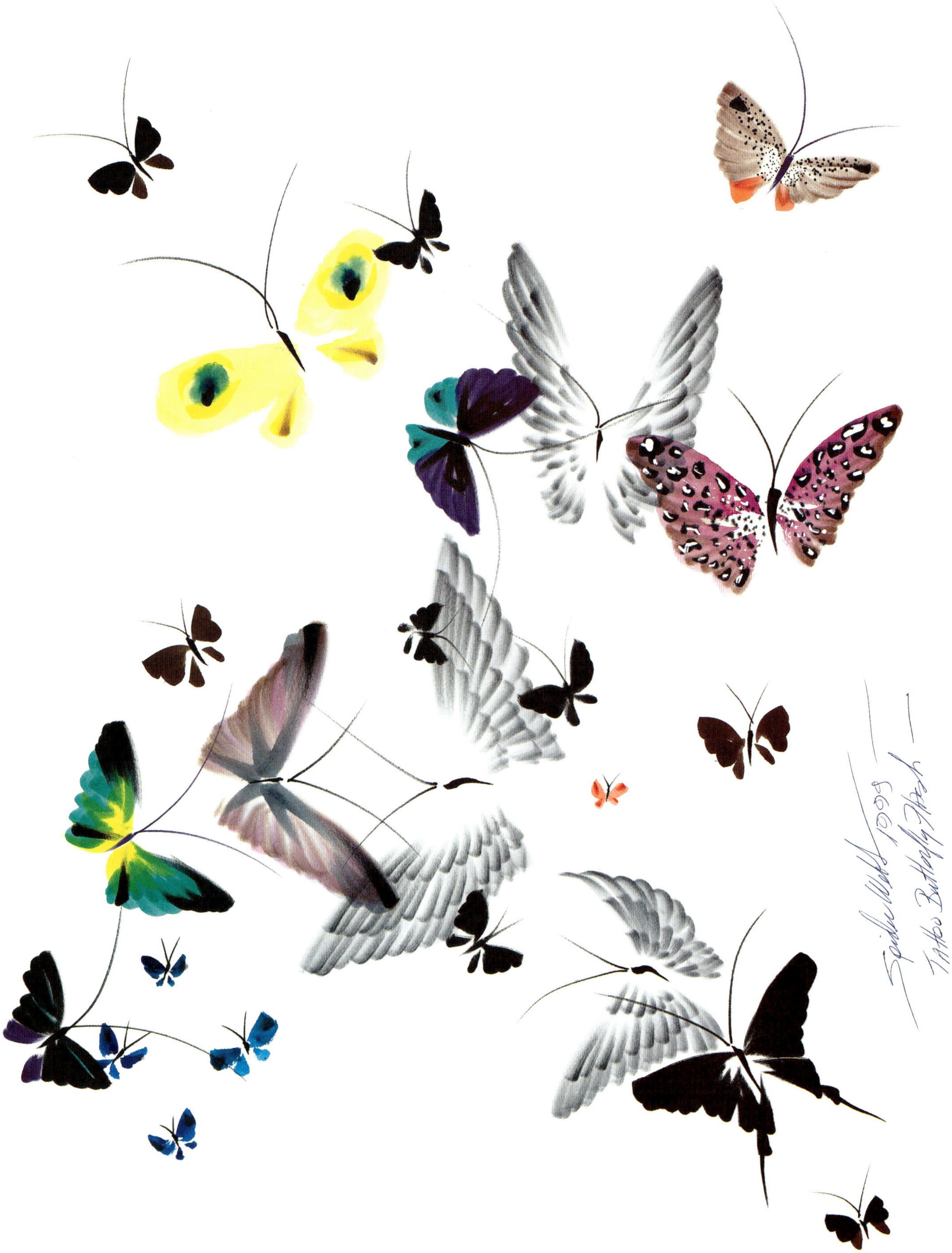
Spider Webb 1998
Tattoo Butterfly Flash

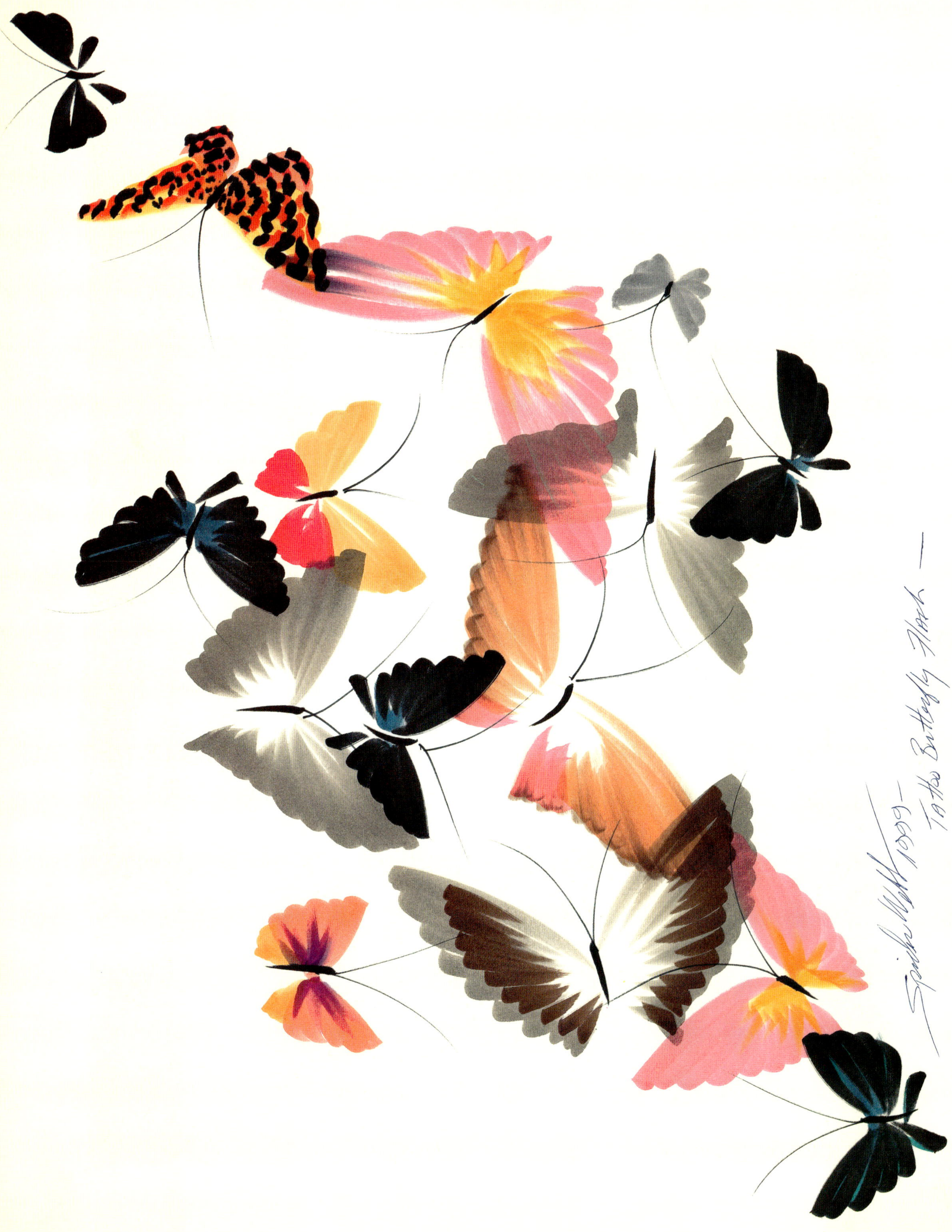
1999
Tattoo Butterfly Flock

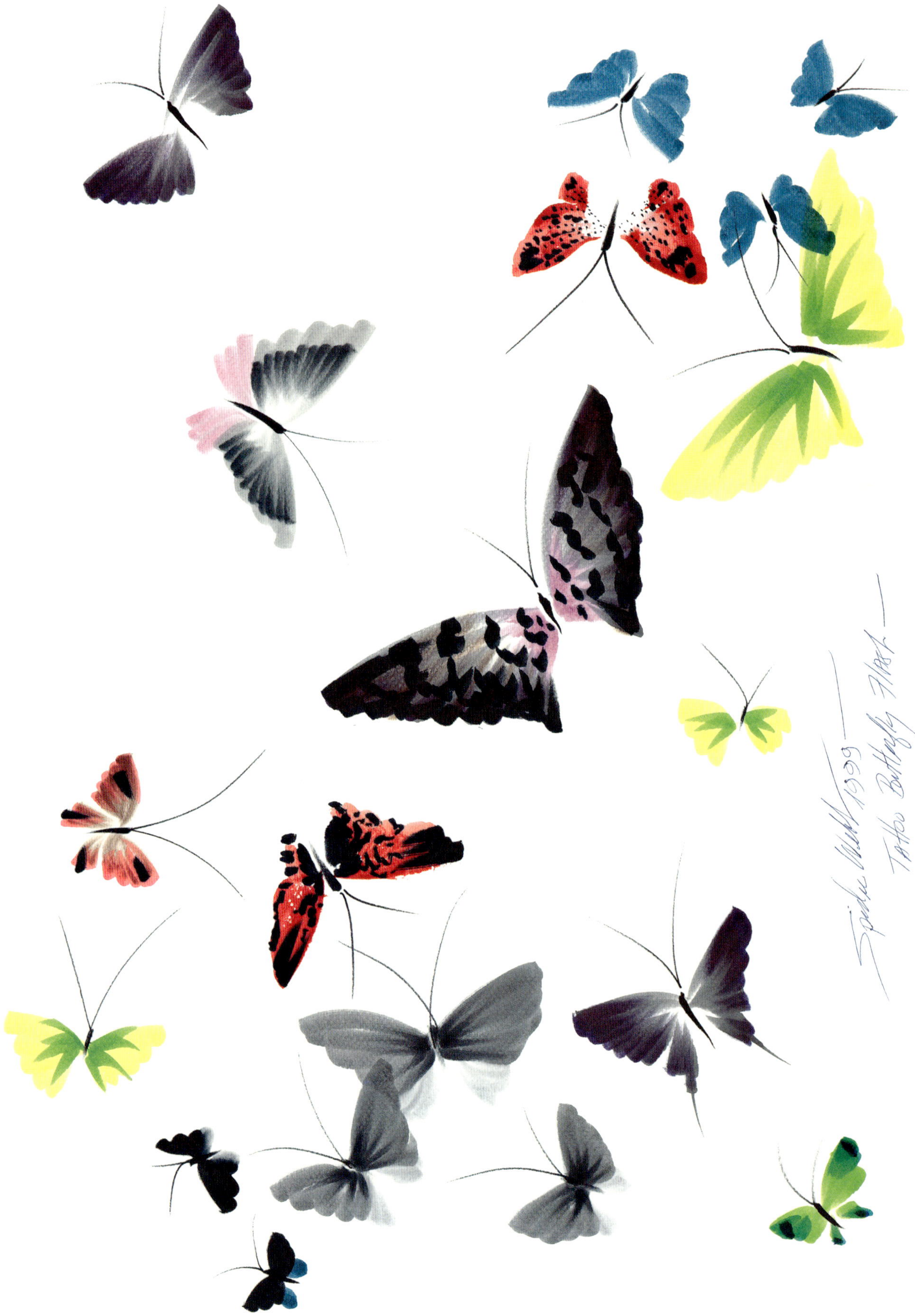

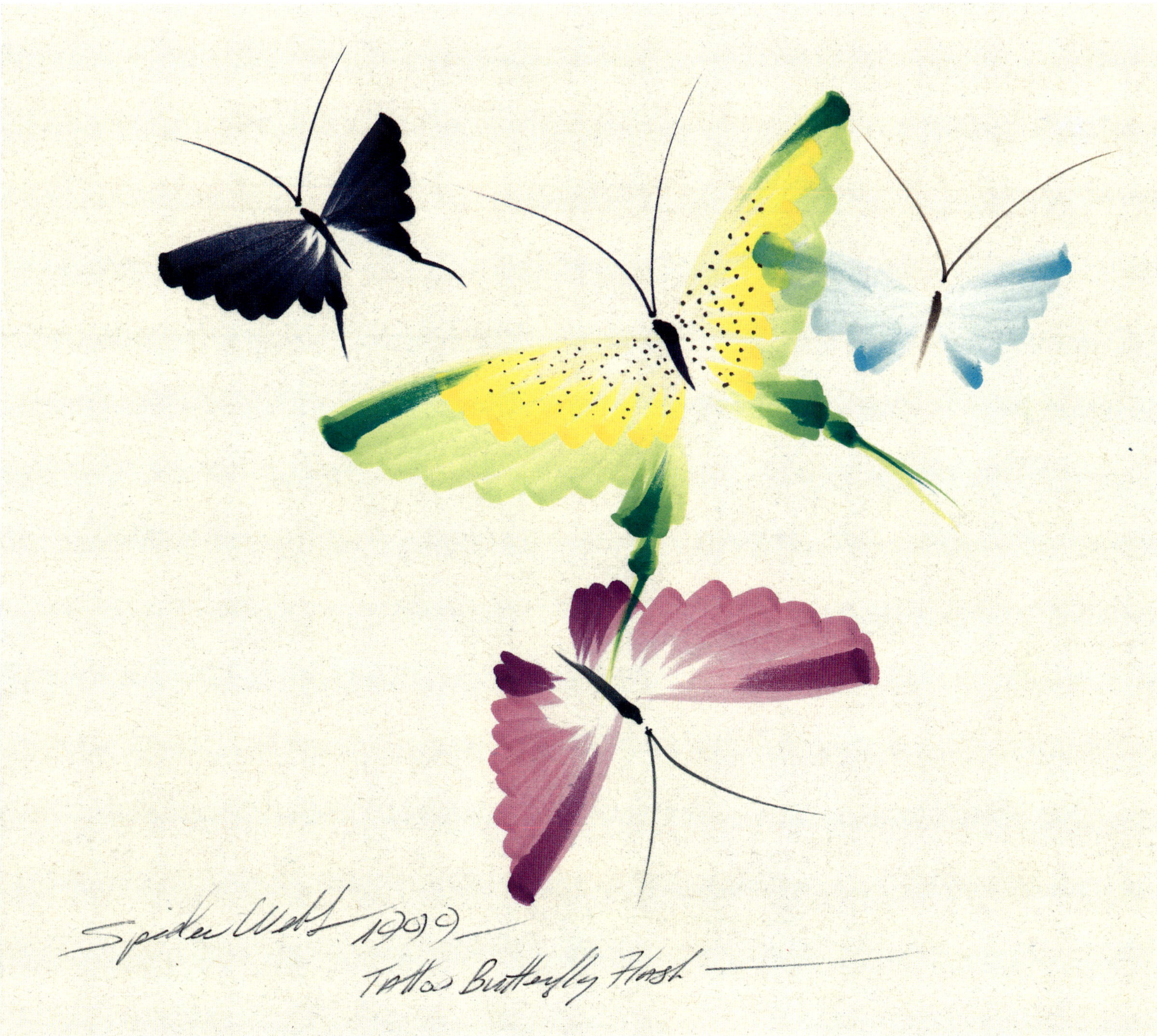
1999
Tattoo Butterfly Flash

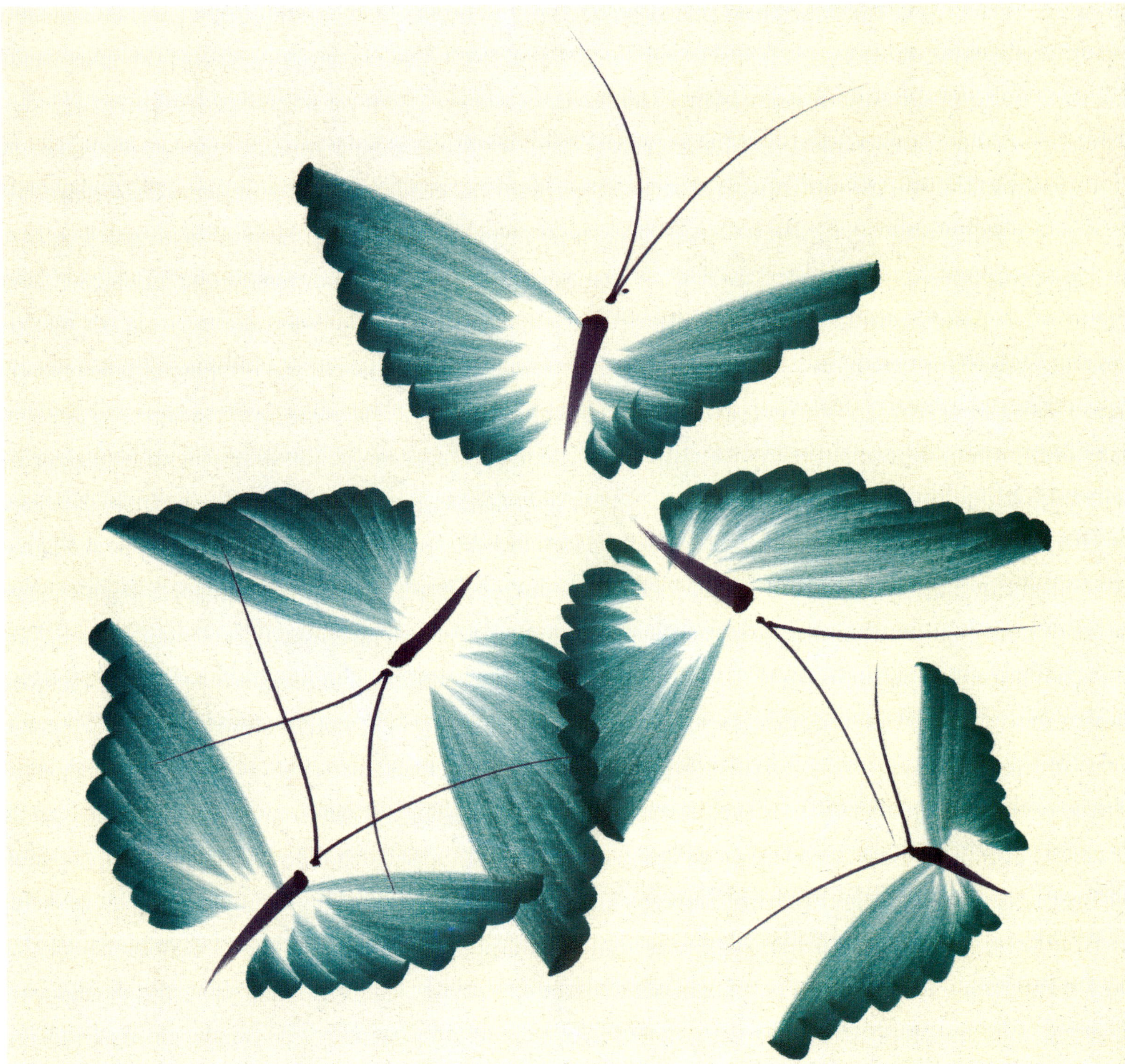

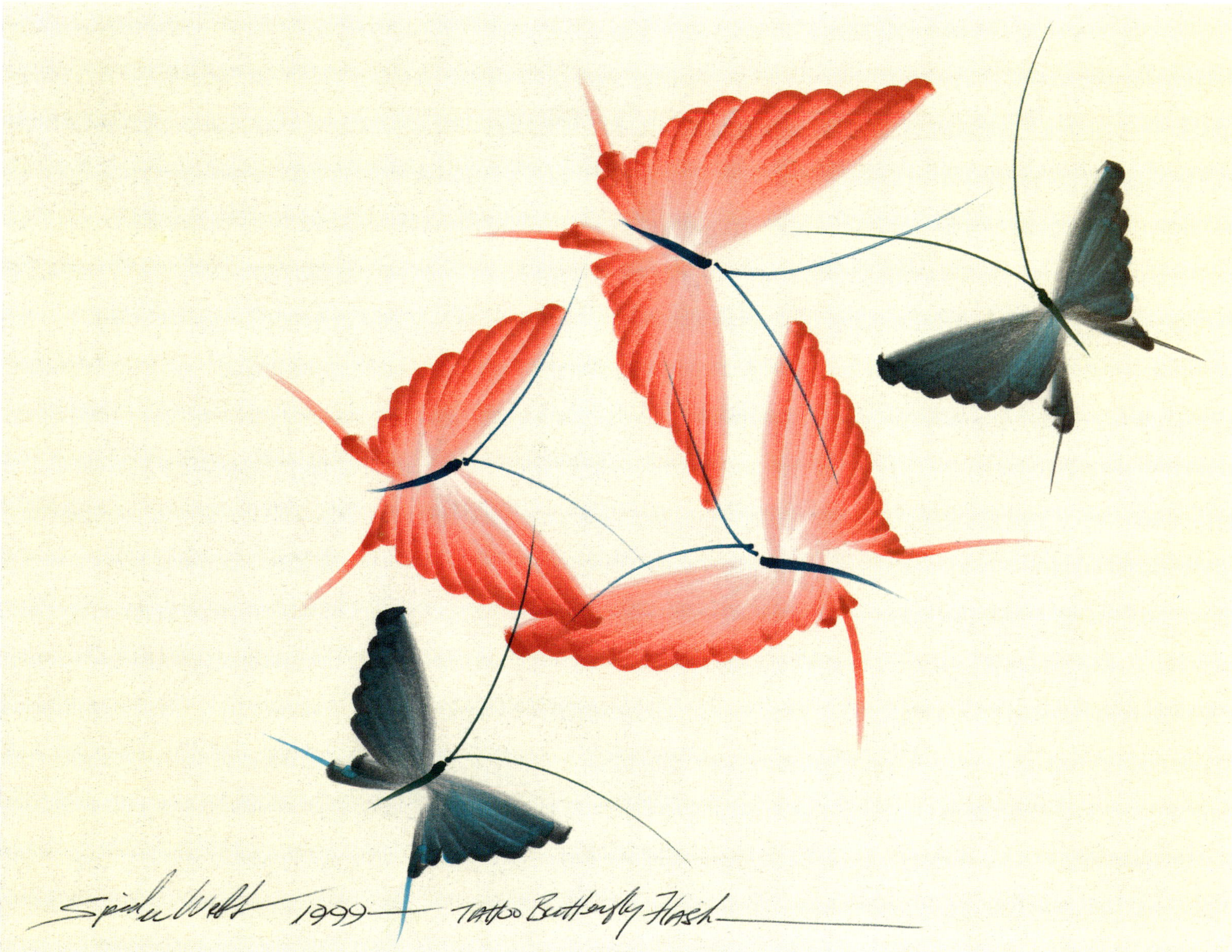
1999 Tattoo Butterfly Flash

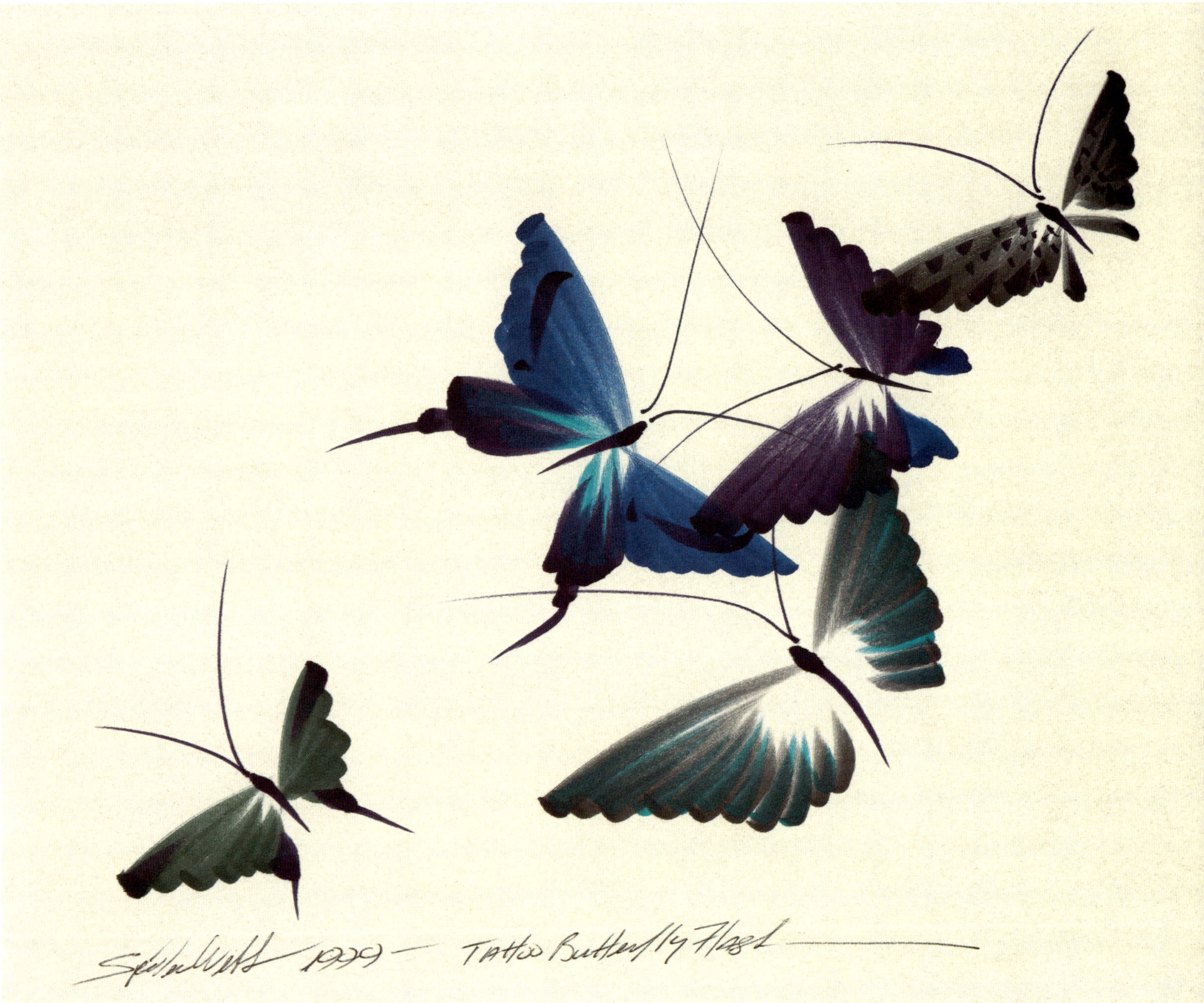
1999 – Tattoo Butterfly Flash

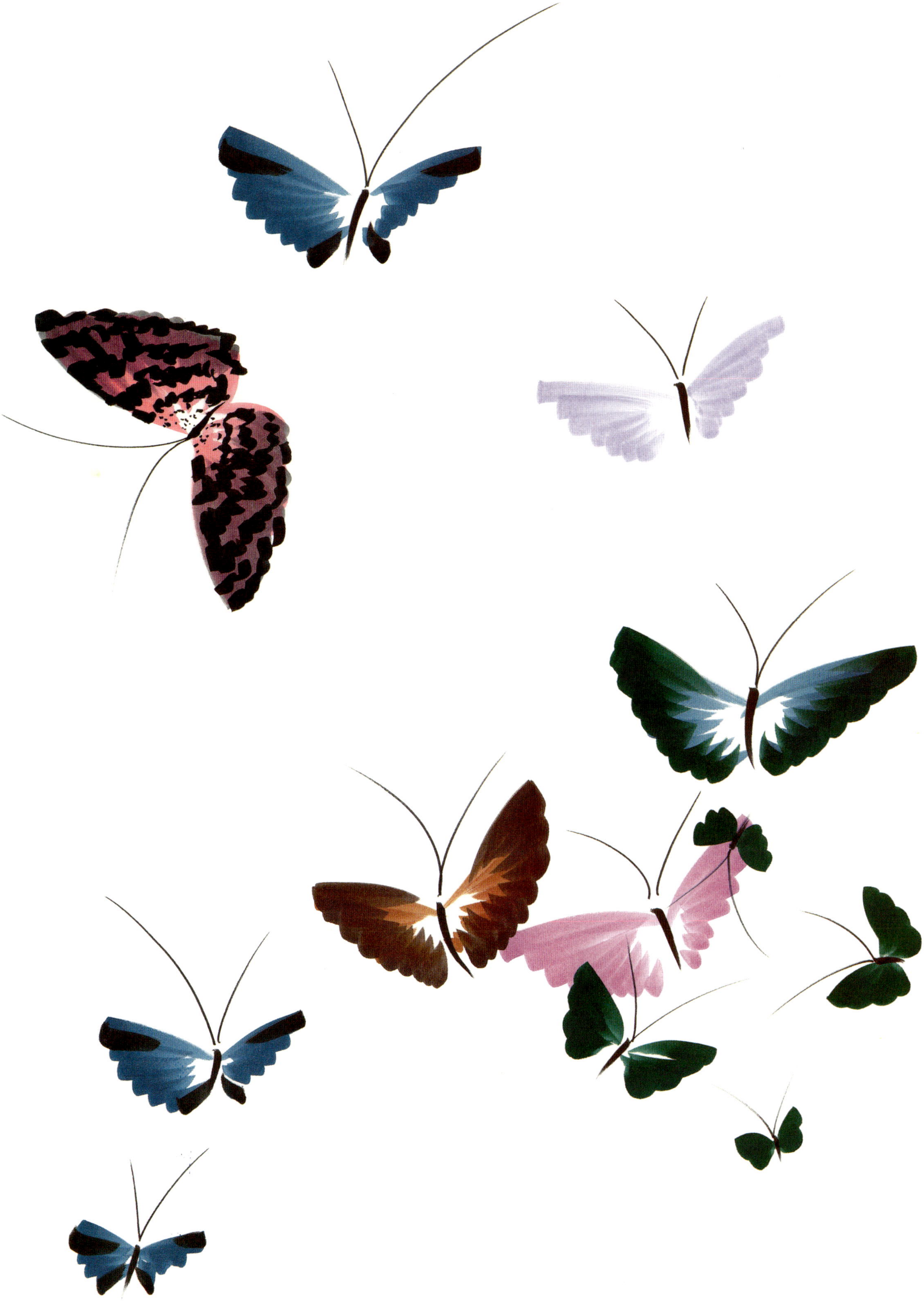

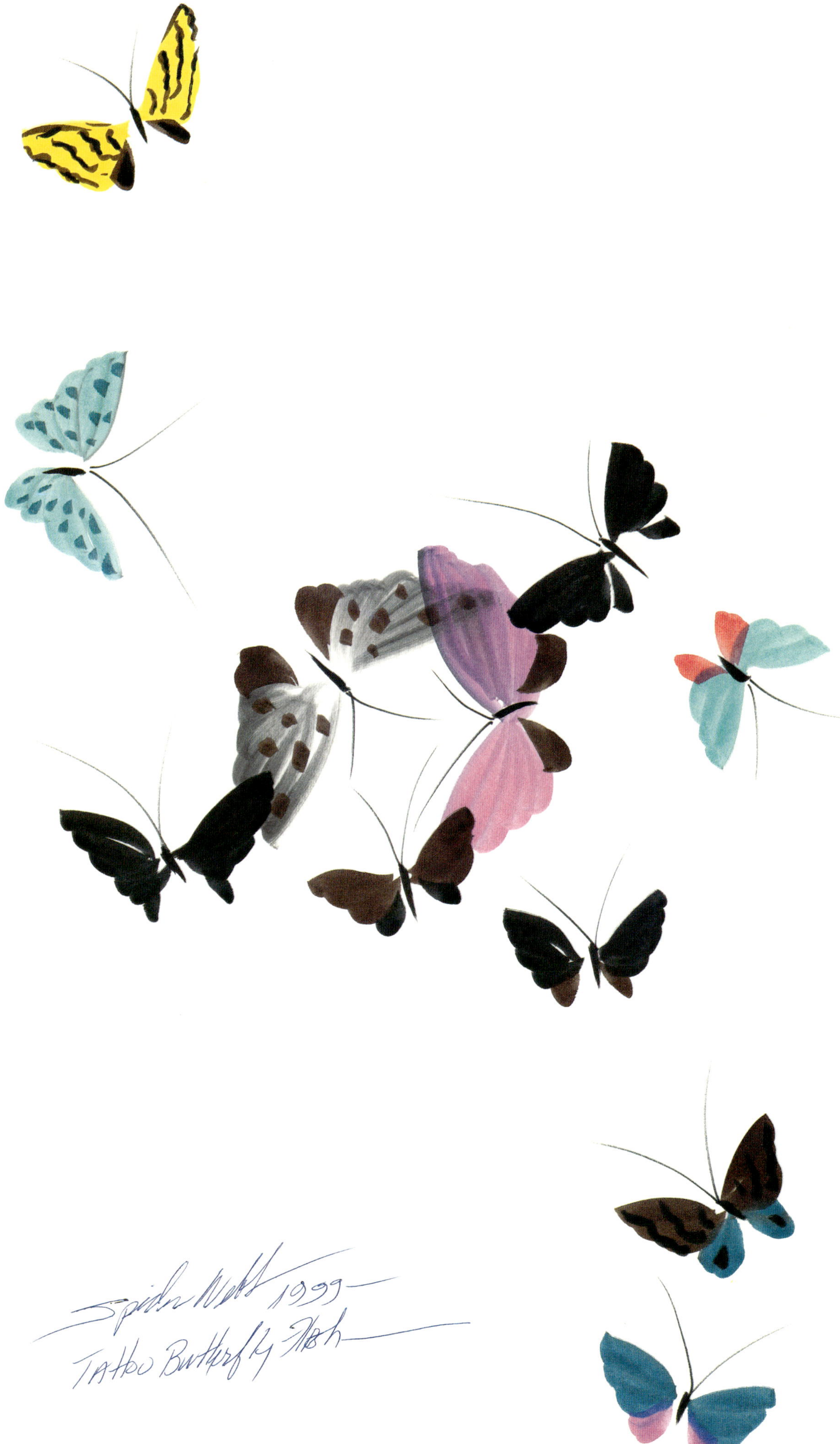
Spider Webb 1999
Tattoo Butterfly Flash

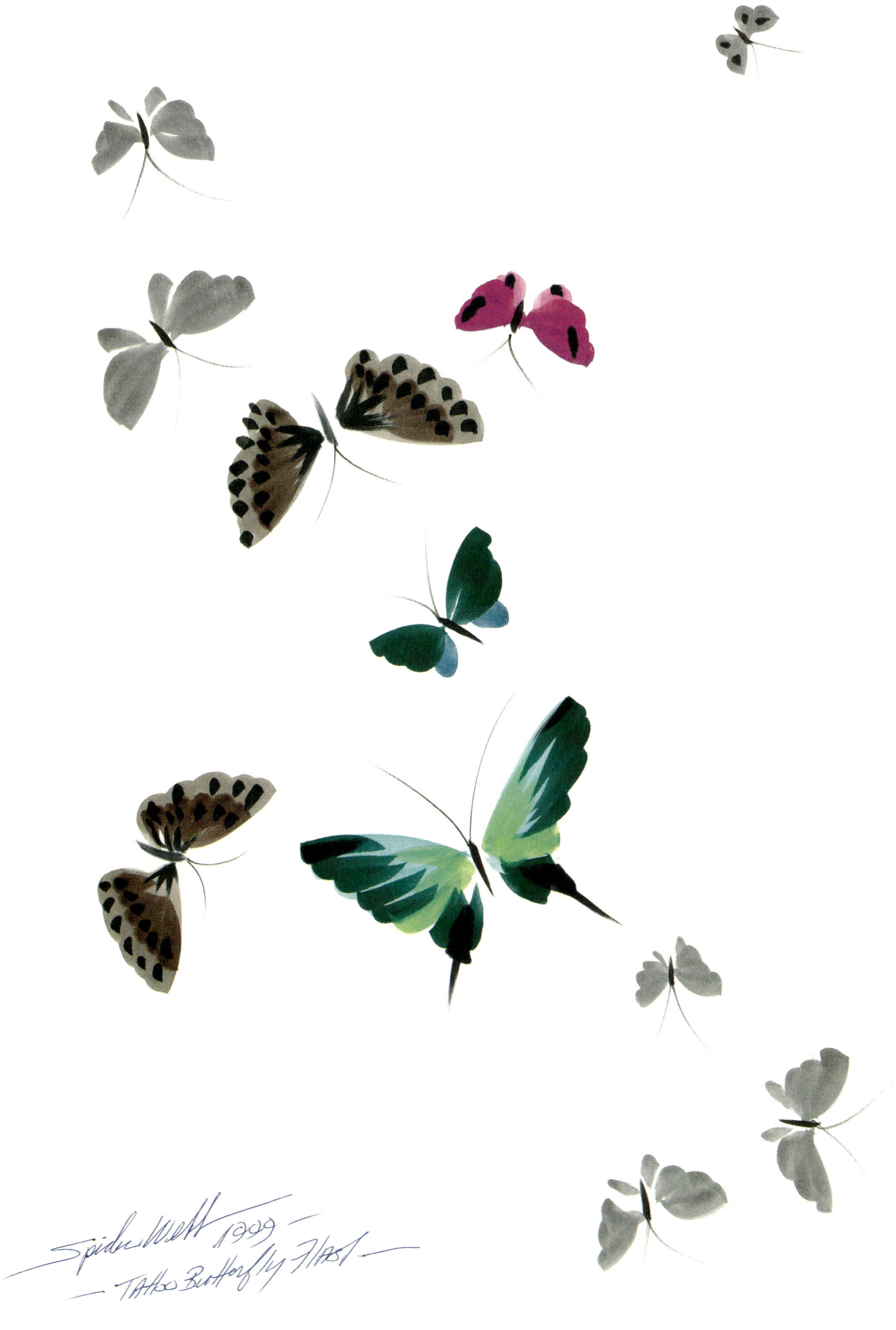
Spider Webb 1999
Tattoo Butterfly Flash

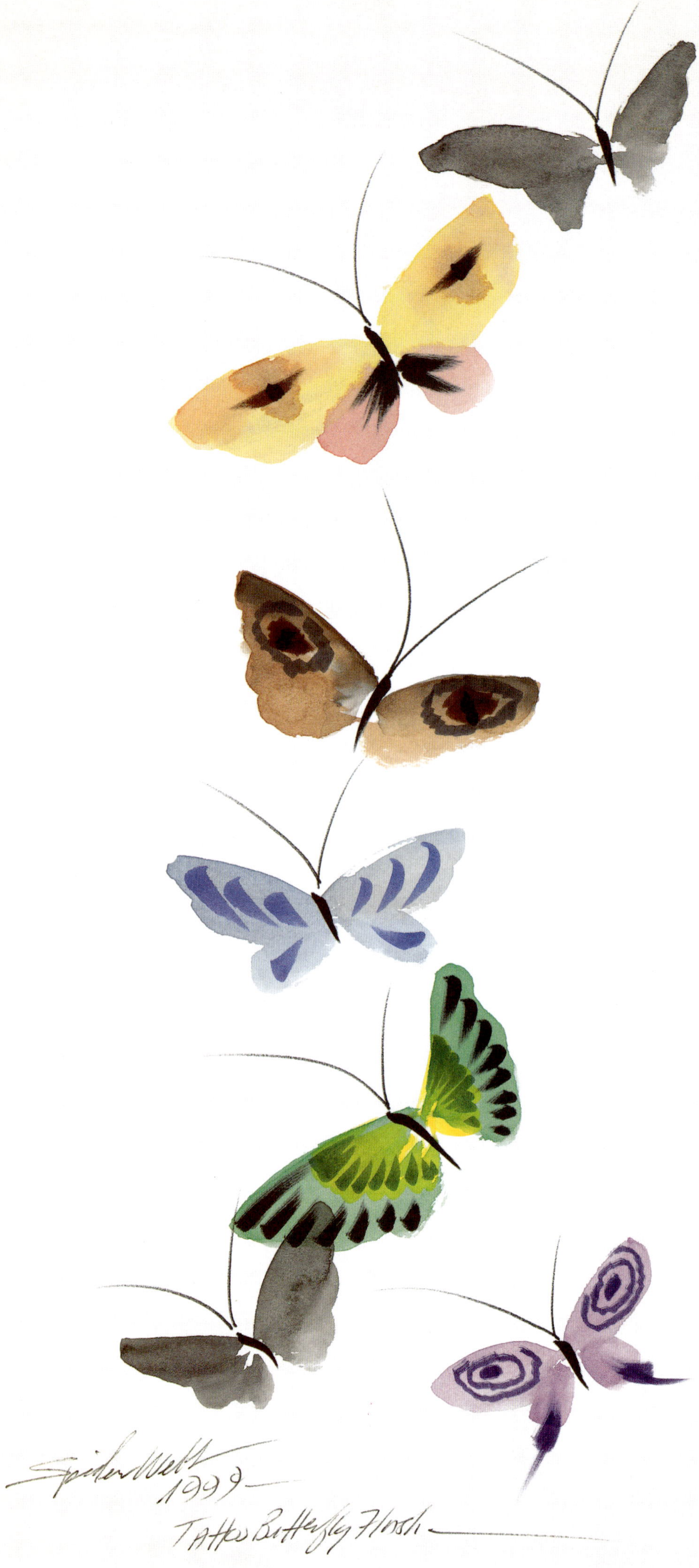
Spider Webb
1999
Tattoo Butterfly Flash

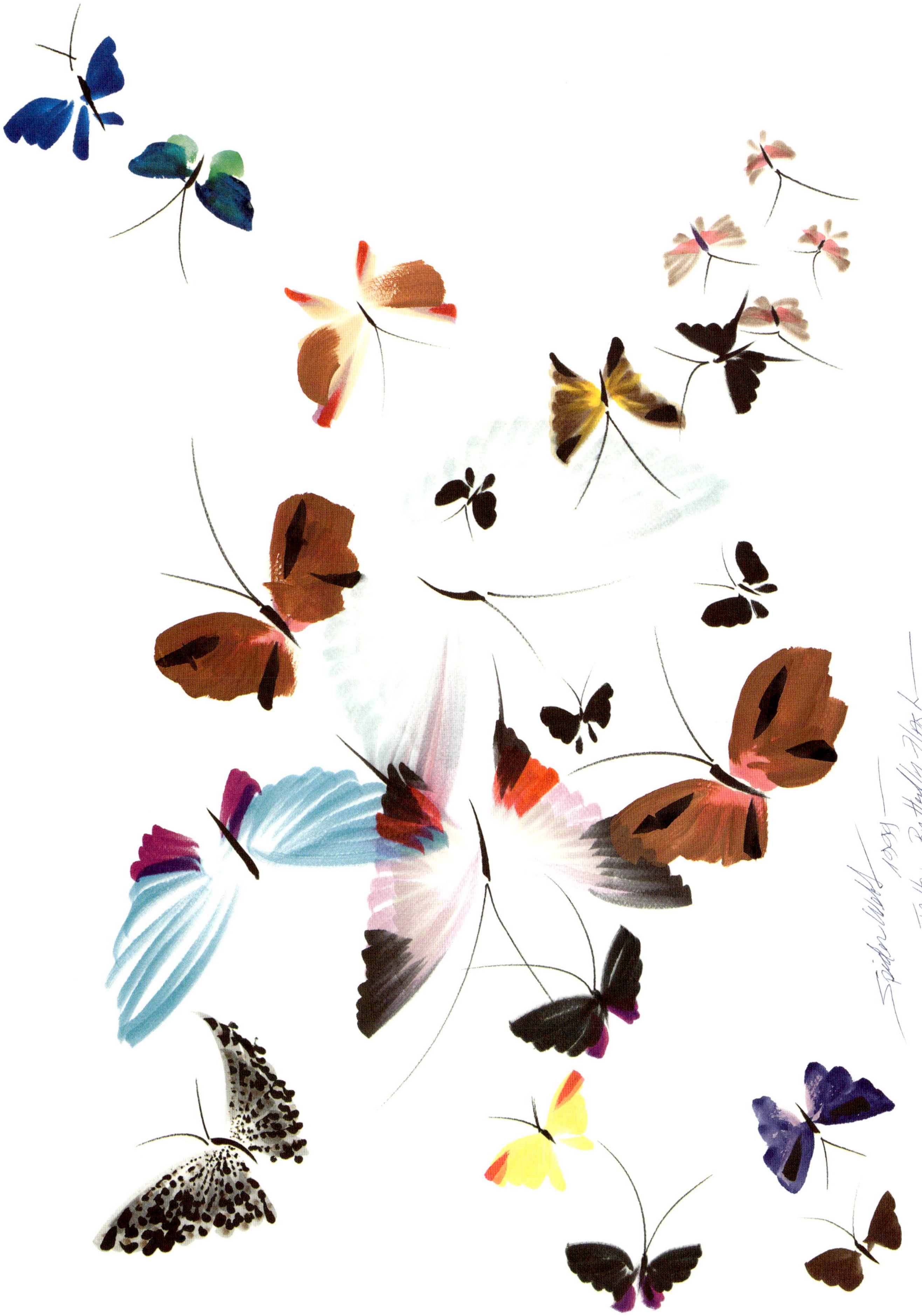

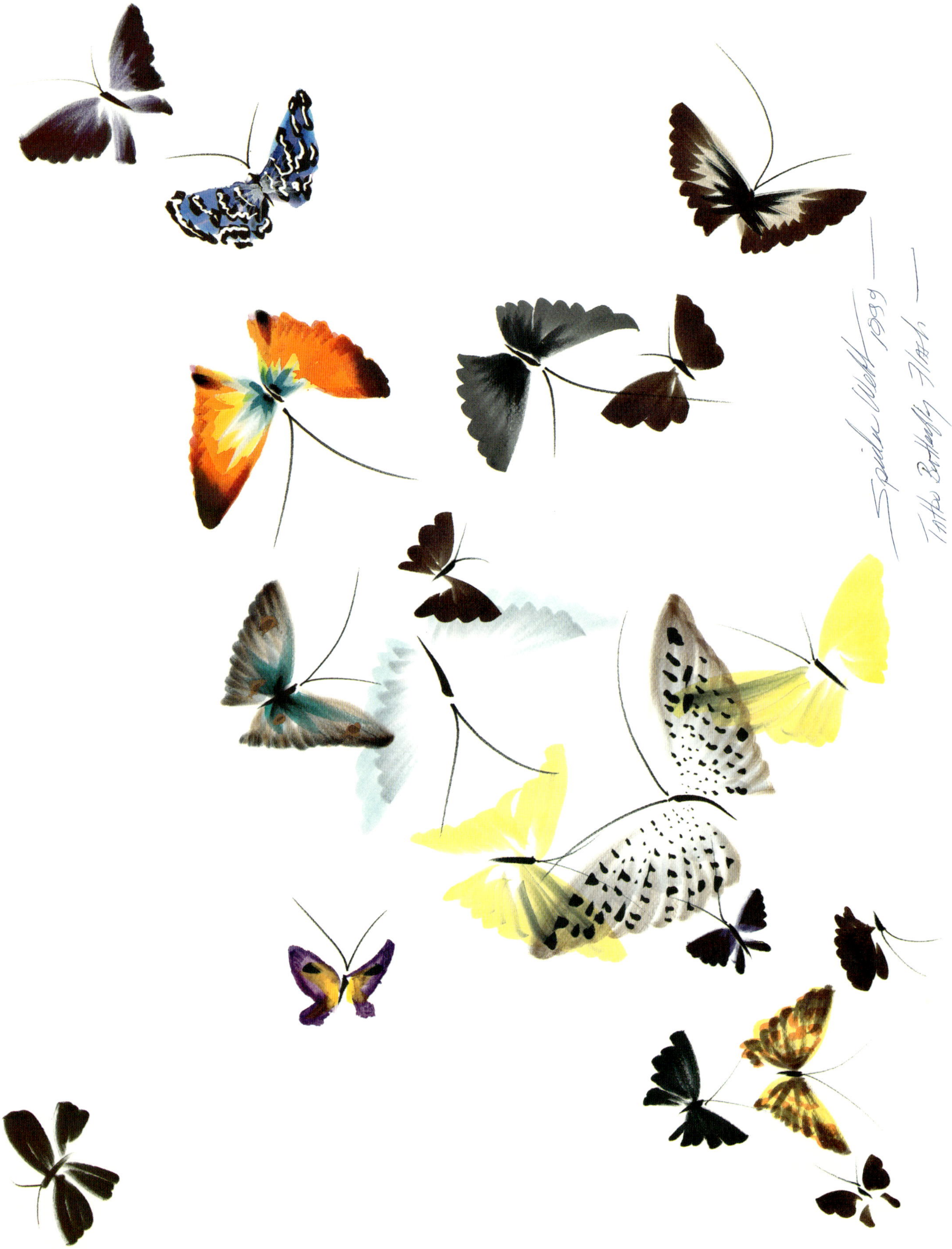
Spider Webb 1989
Tattoo Butterfly Flash

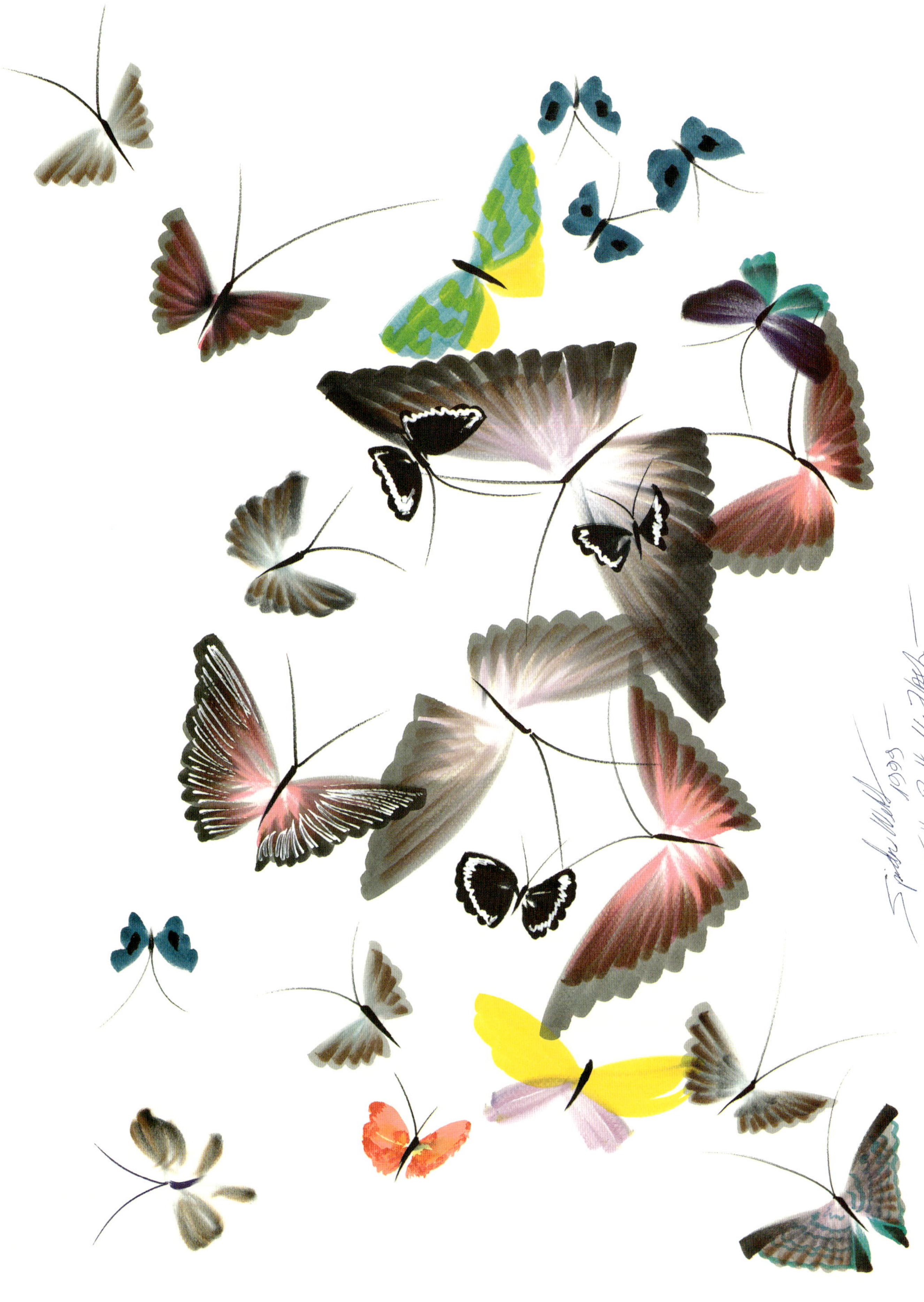

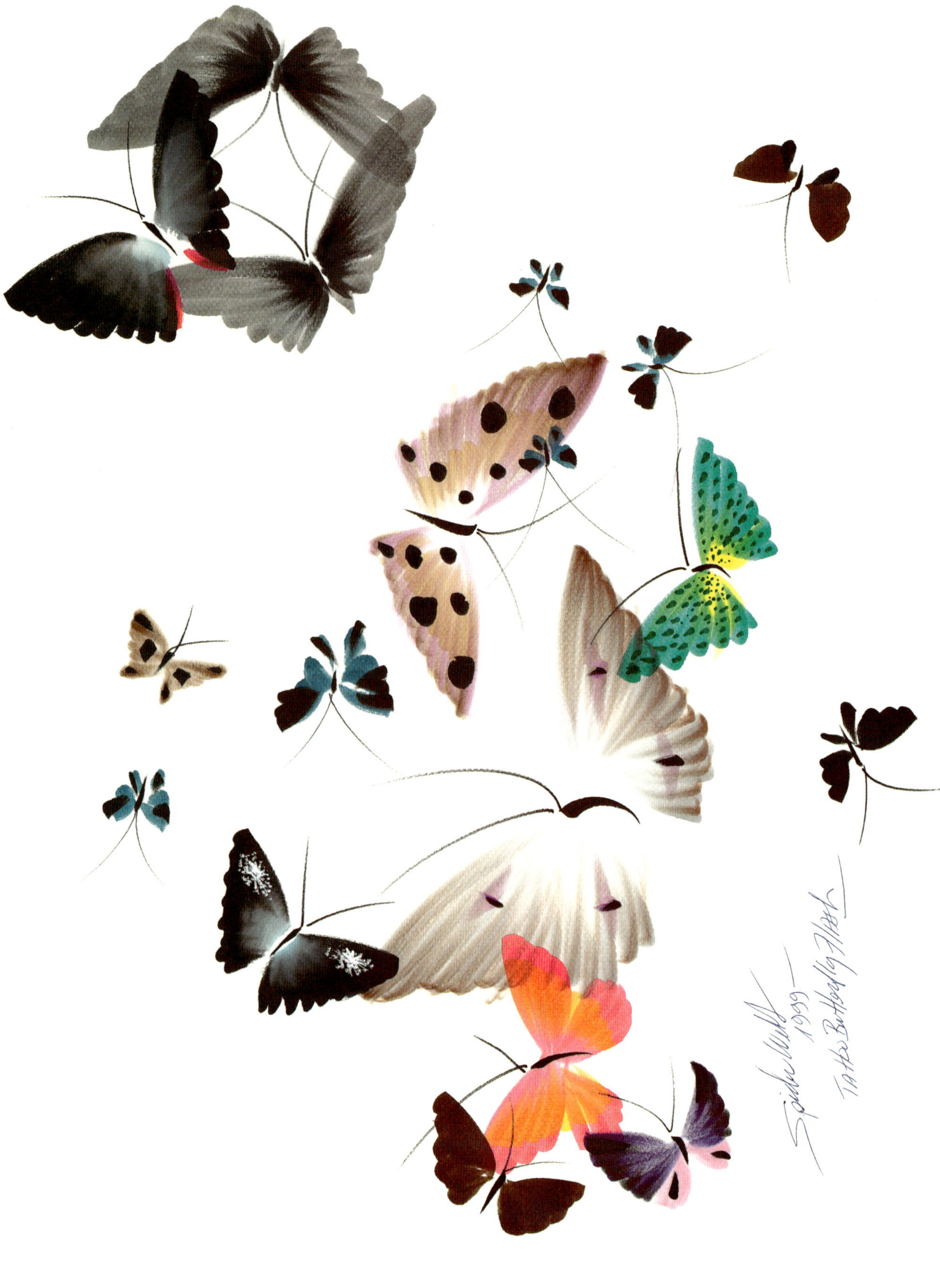

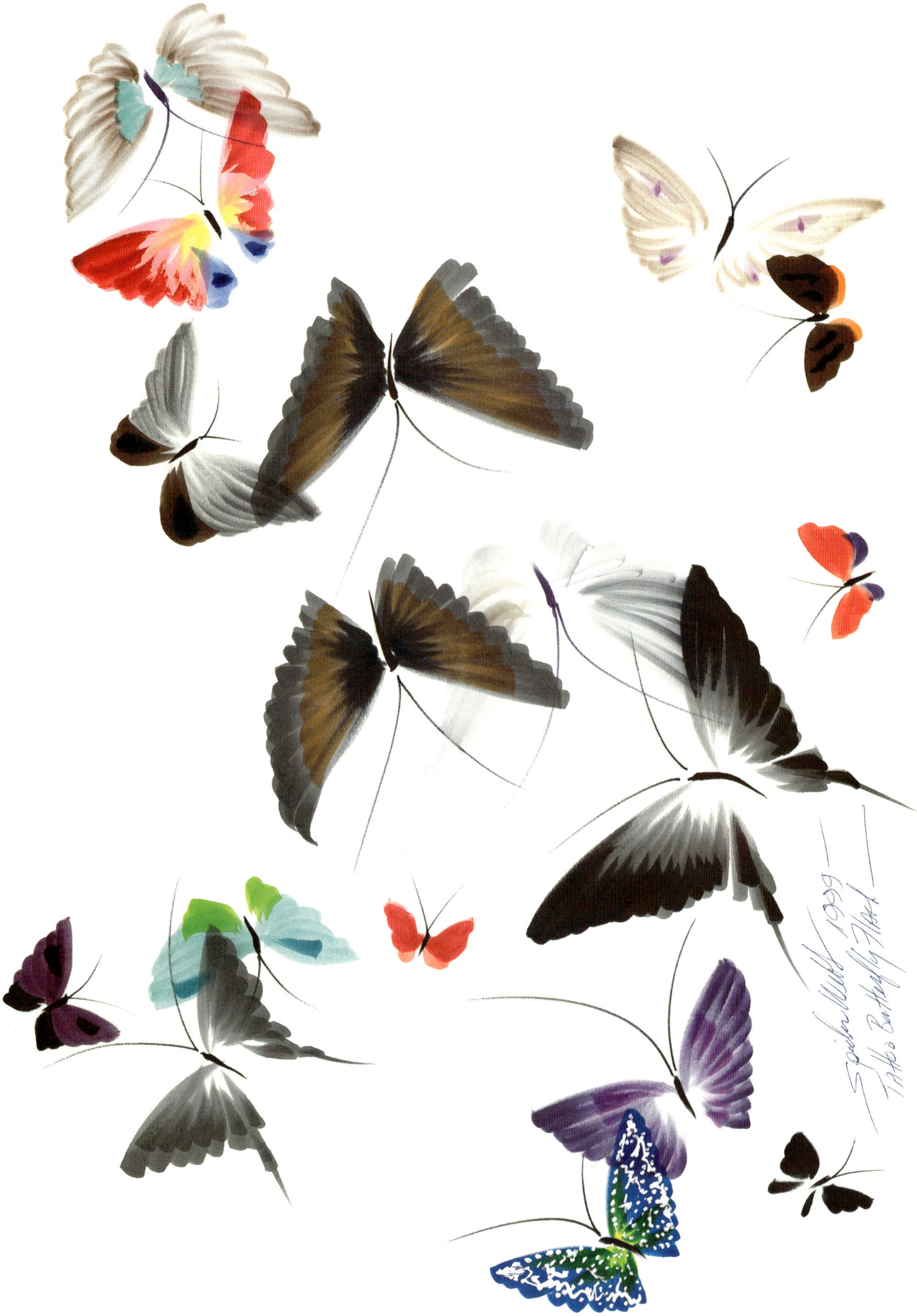

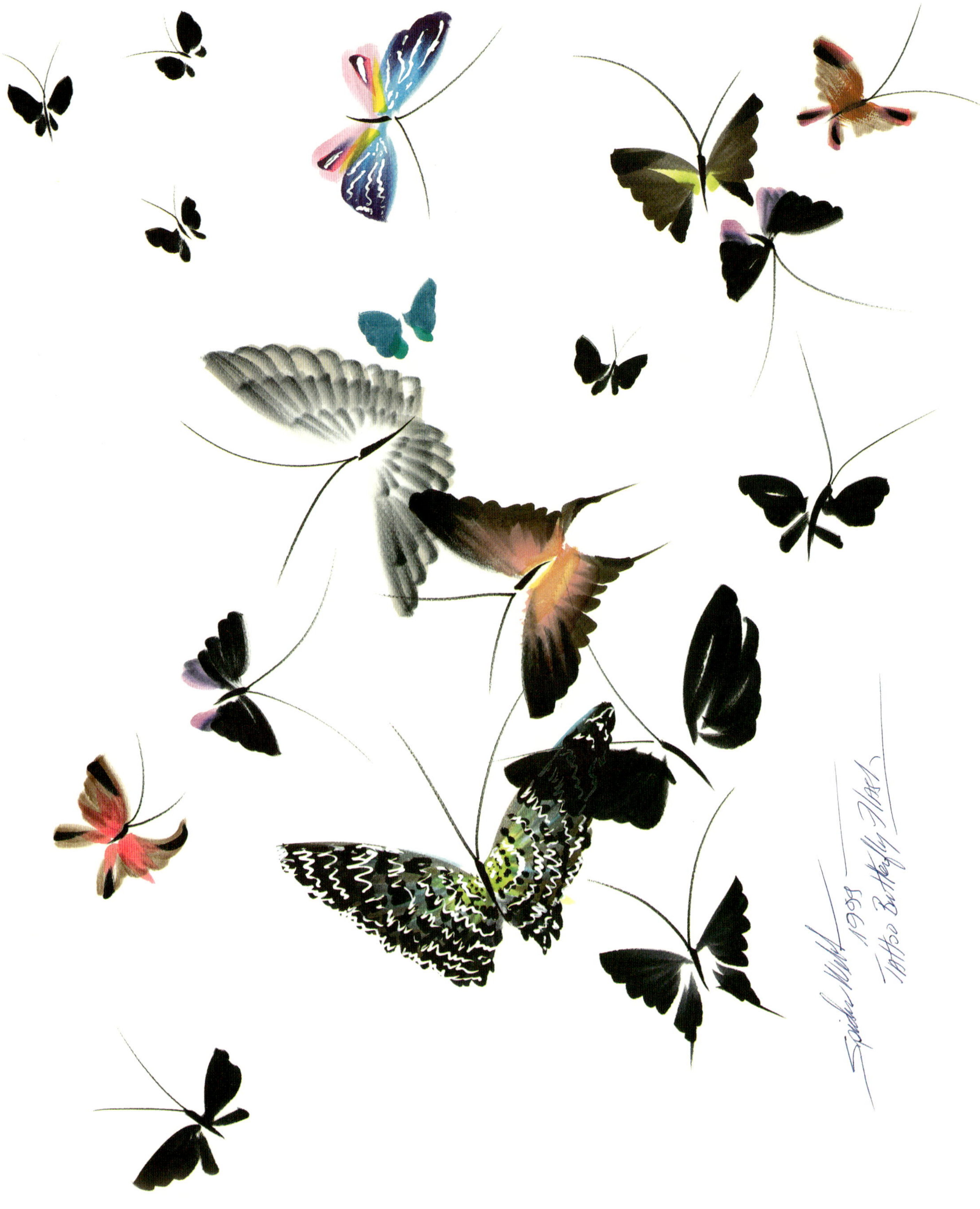

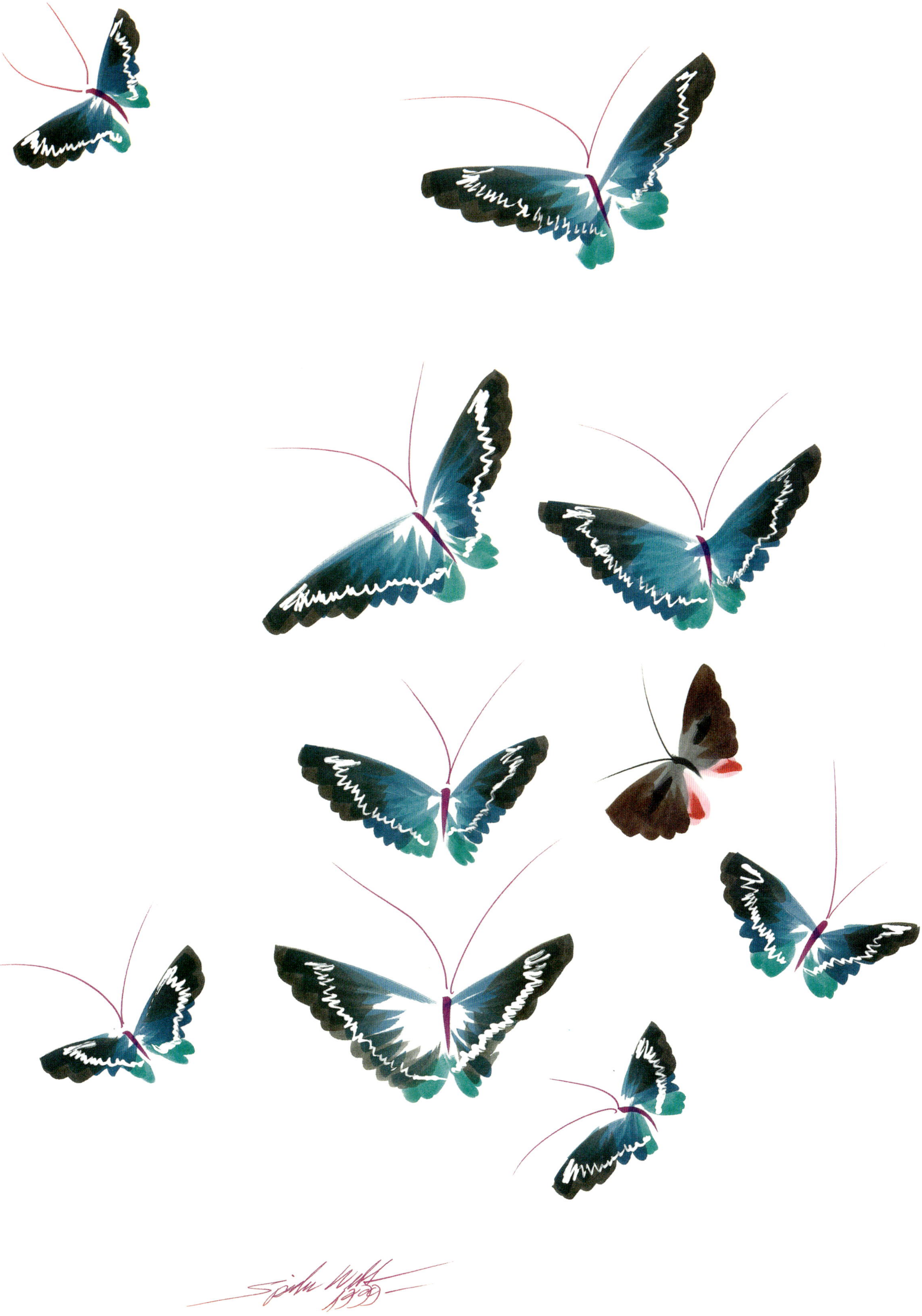

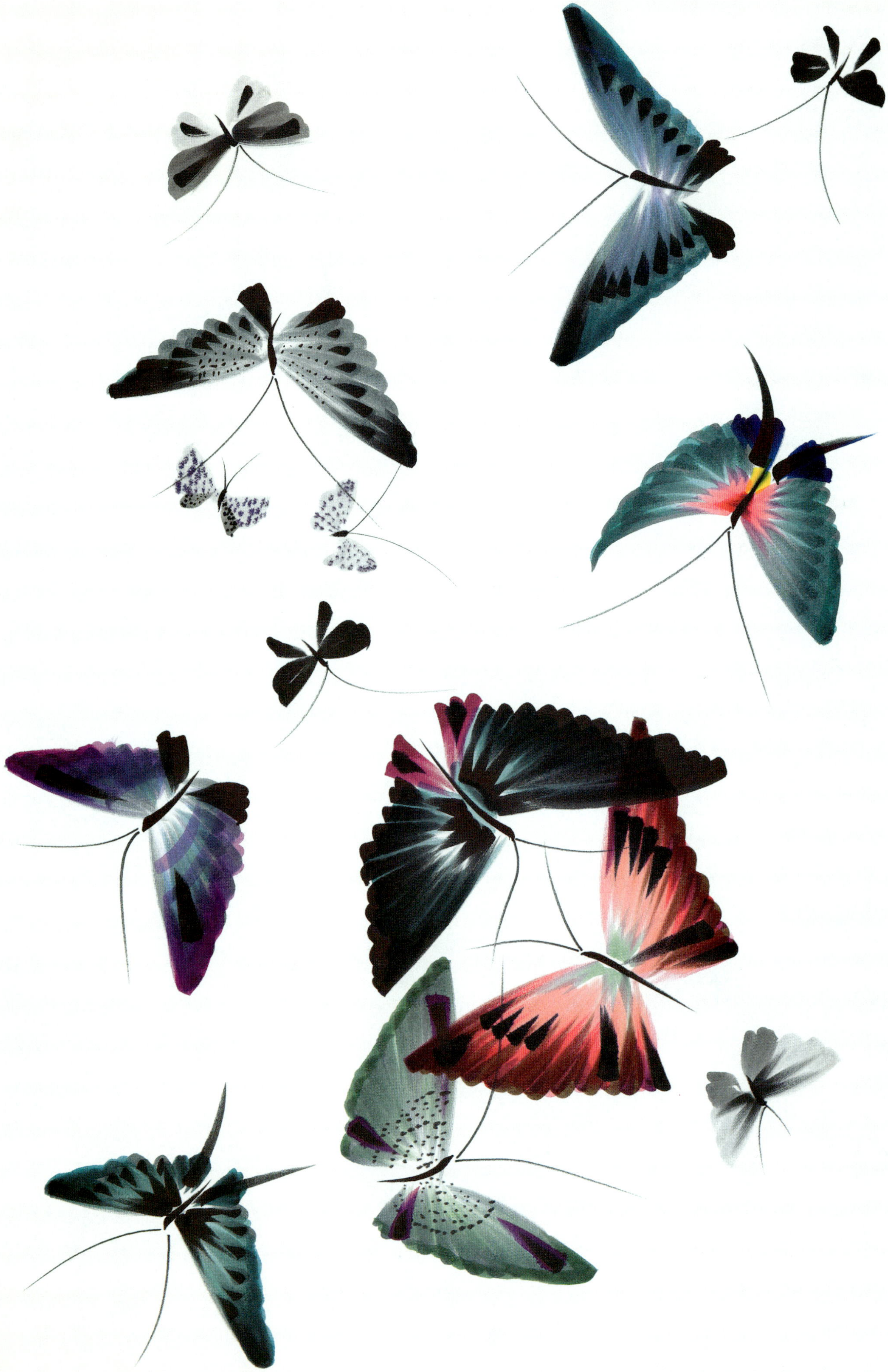

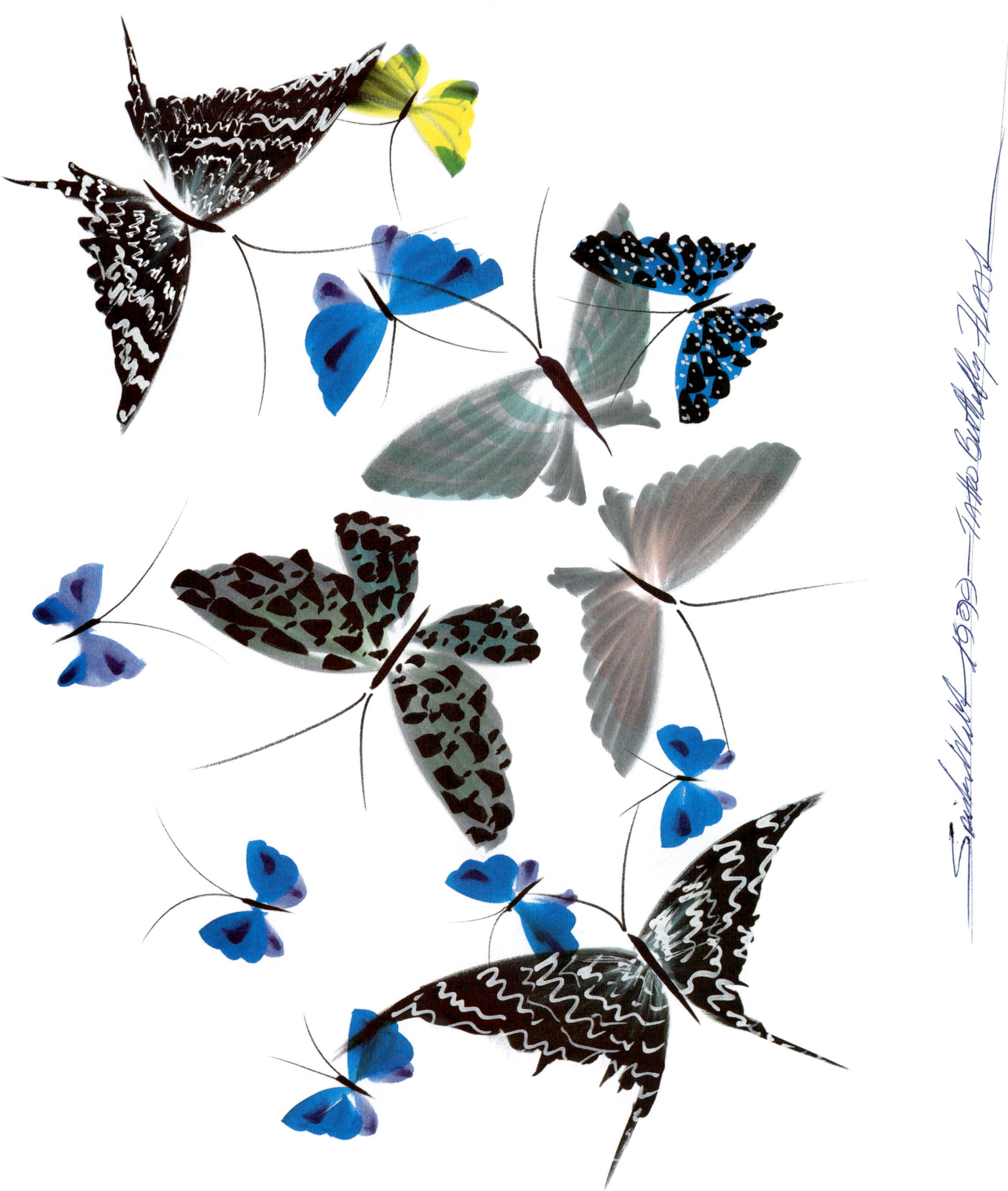

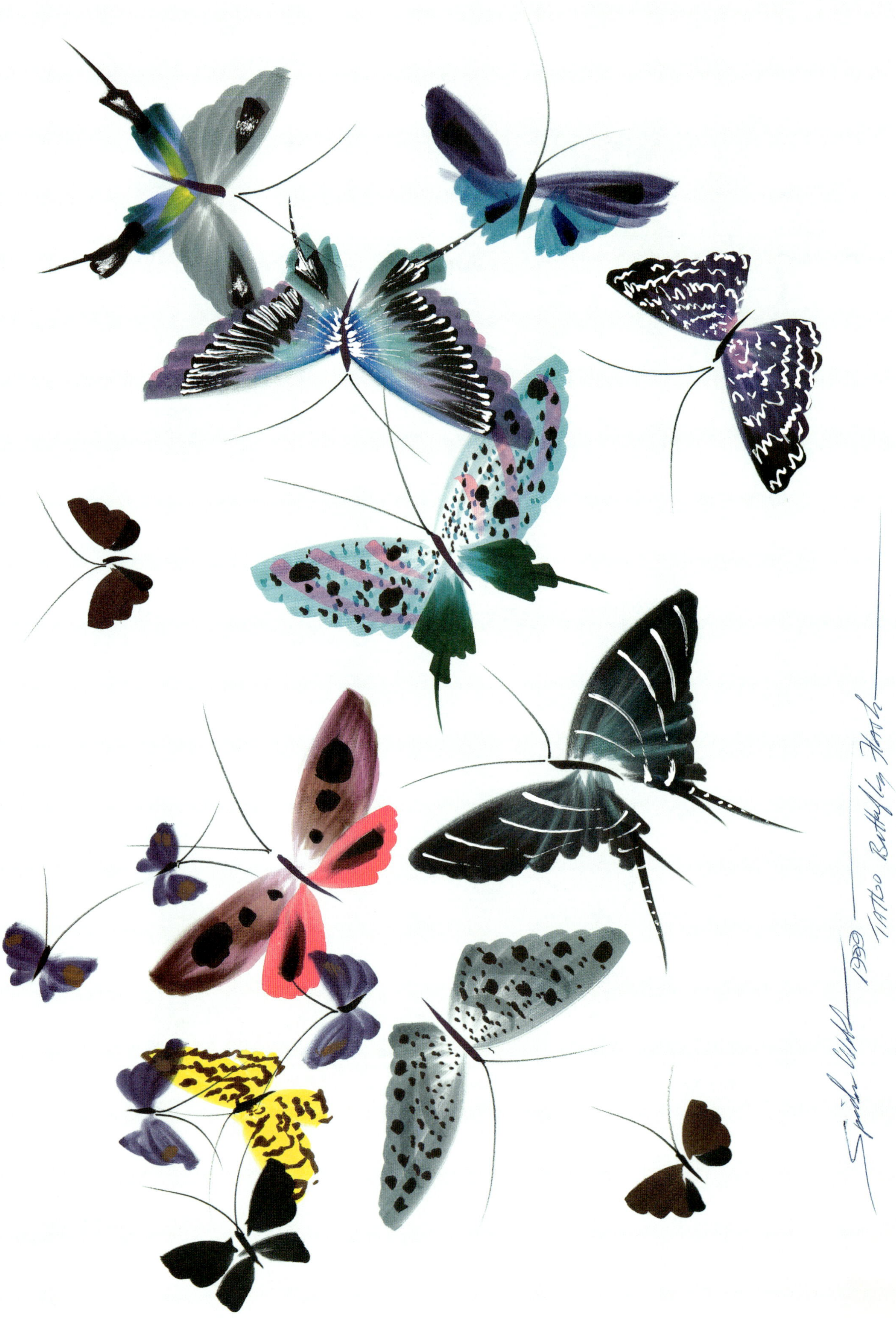
Tattoo Butterfly Flash

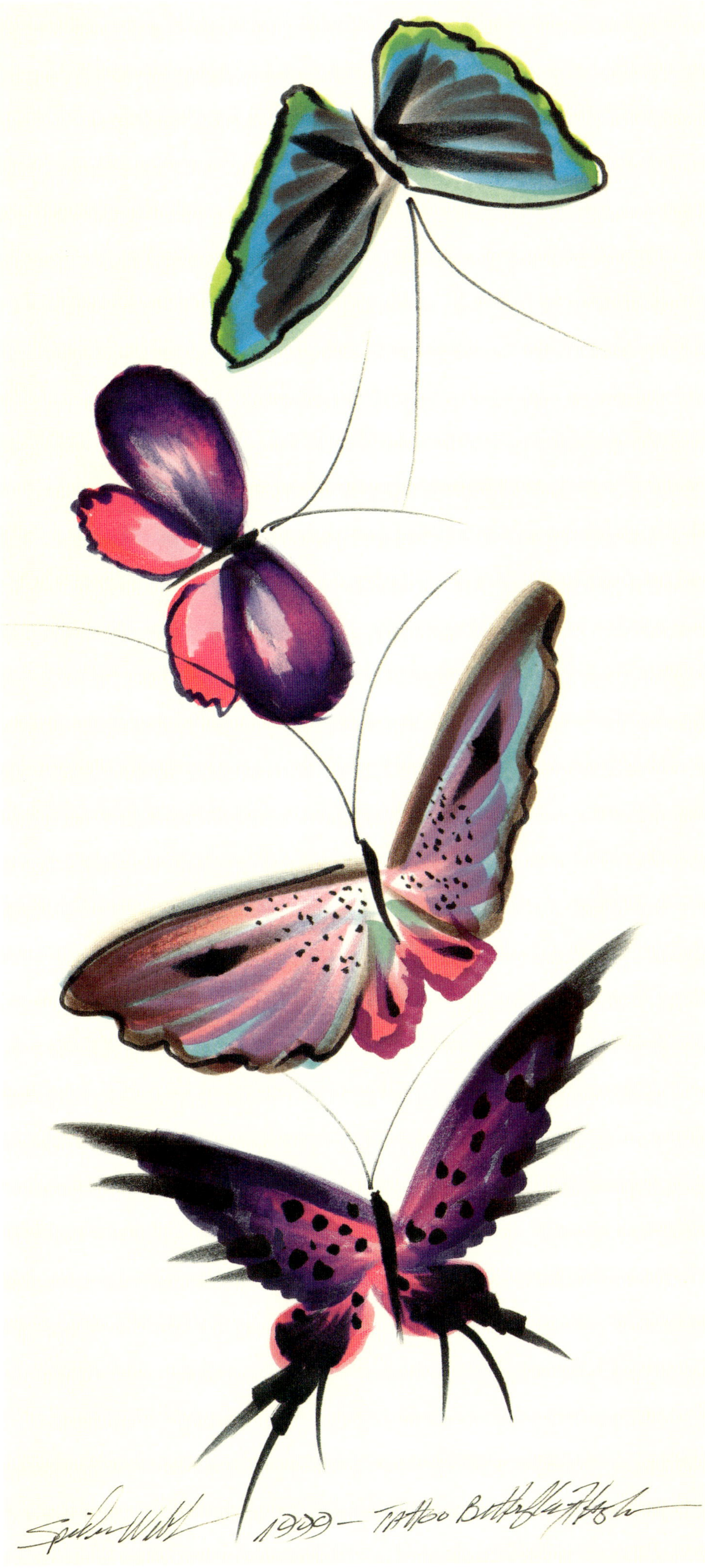
1999 - Tattoo Butterfly Flash

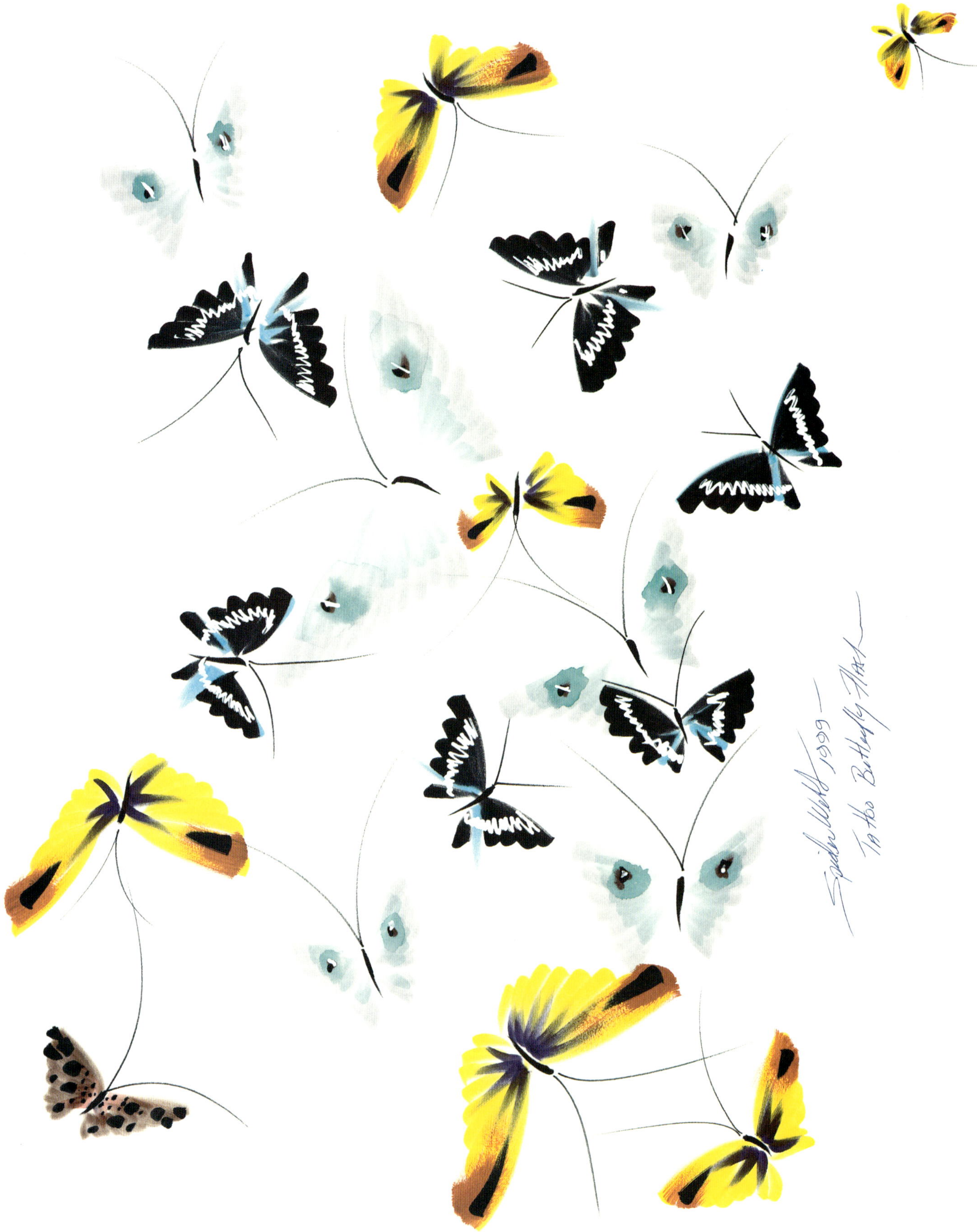
Tattoo Butterfly Flash

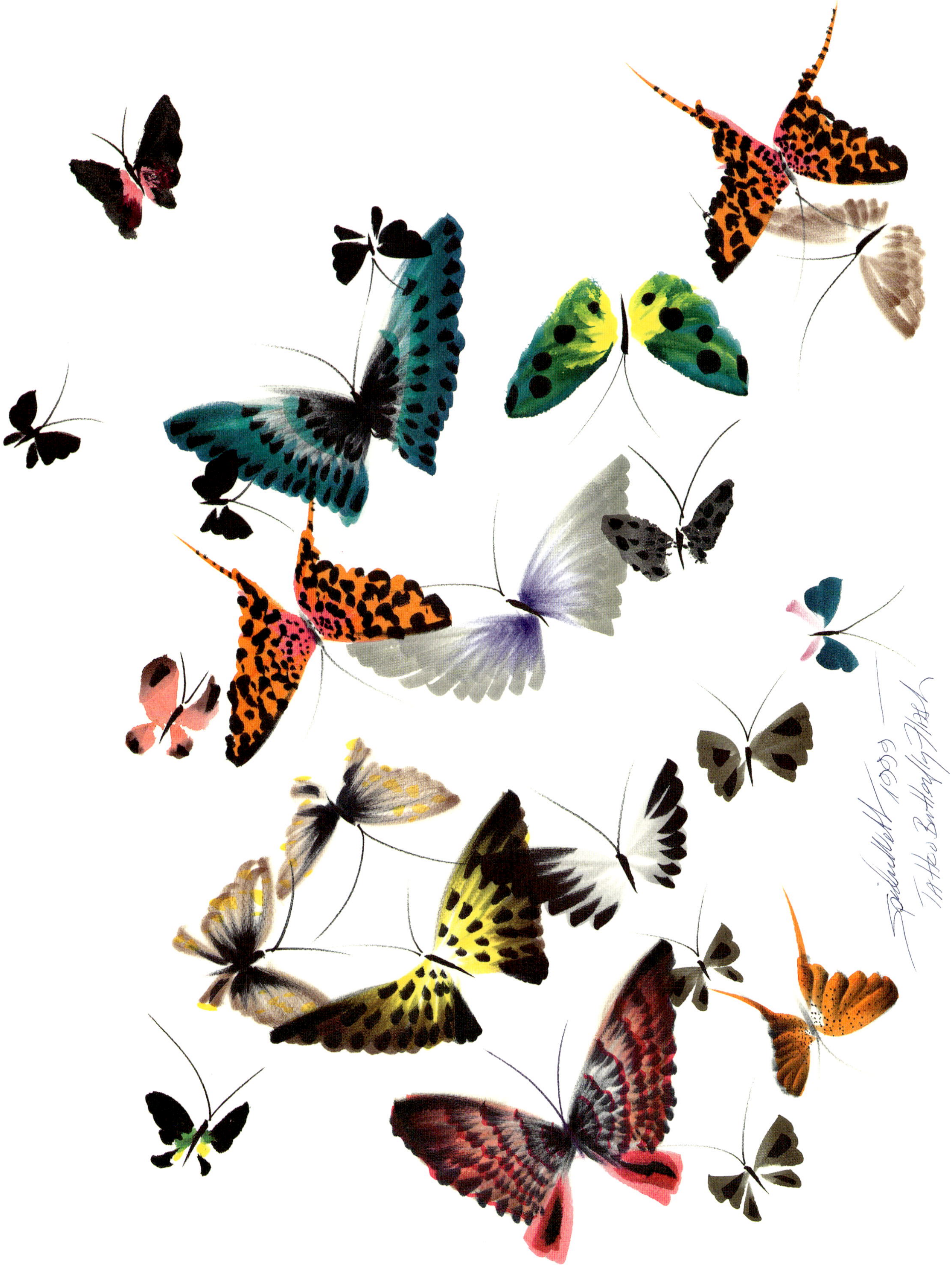
1989
Tattoo Butterfly Flash

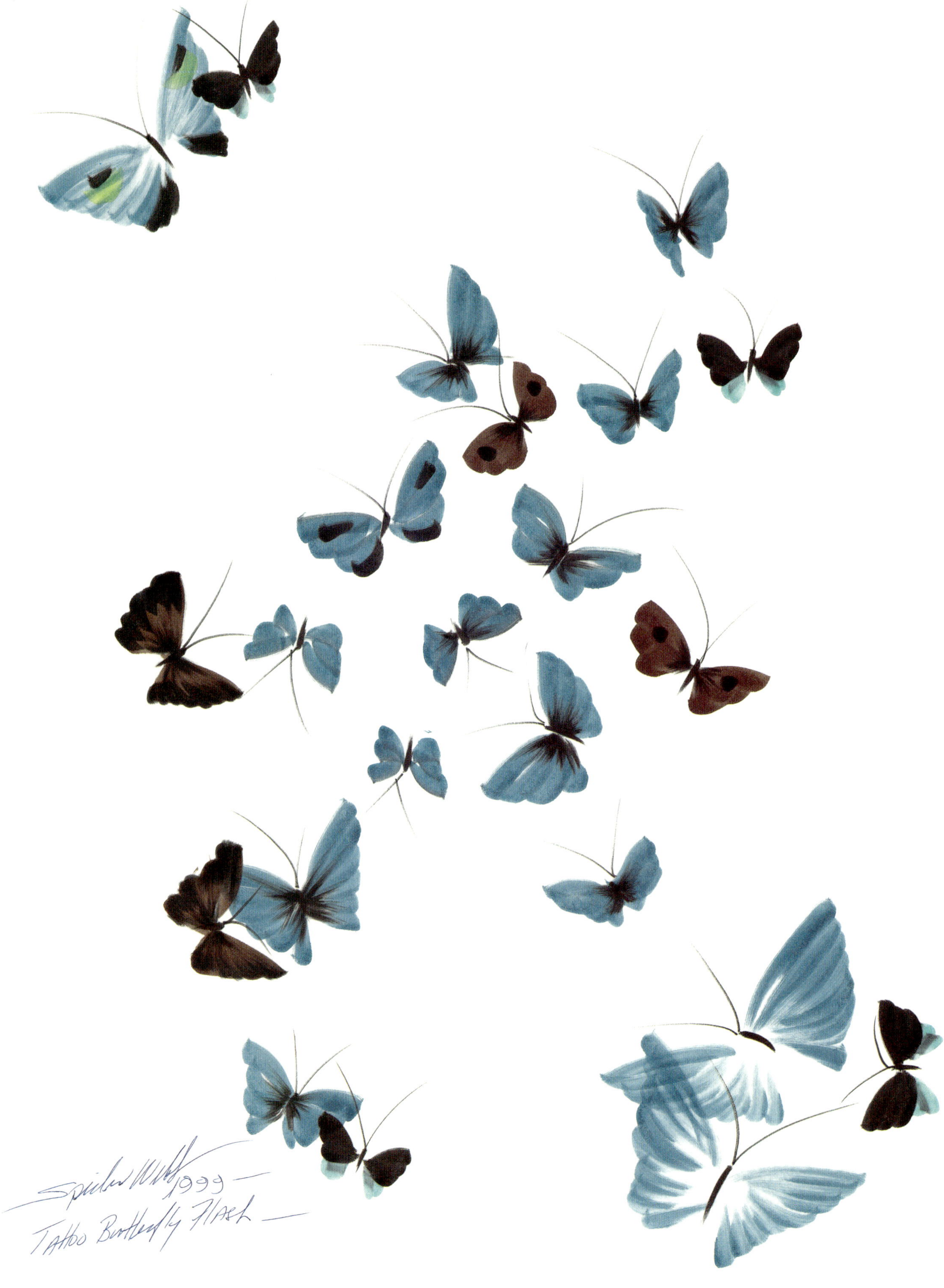
Spider Webb 1999
Tattoo Butterfly Flash

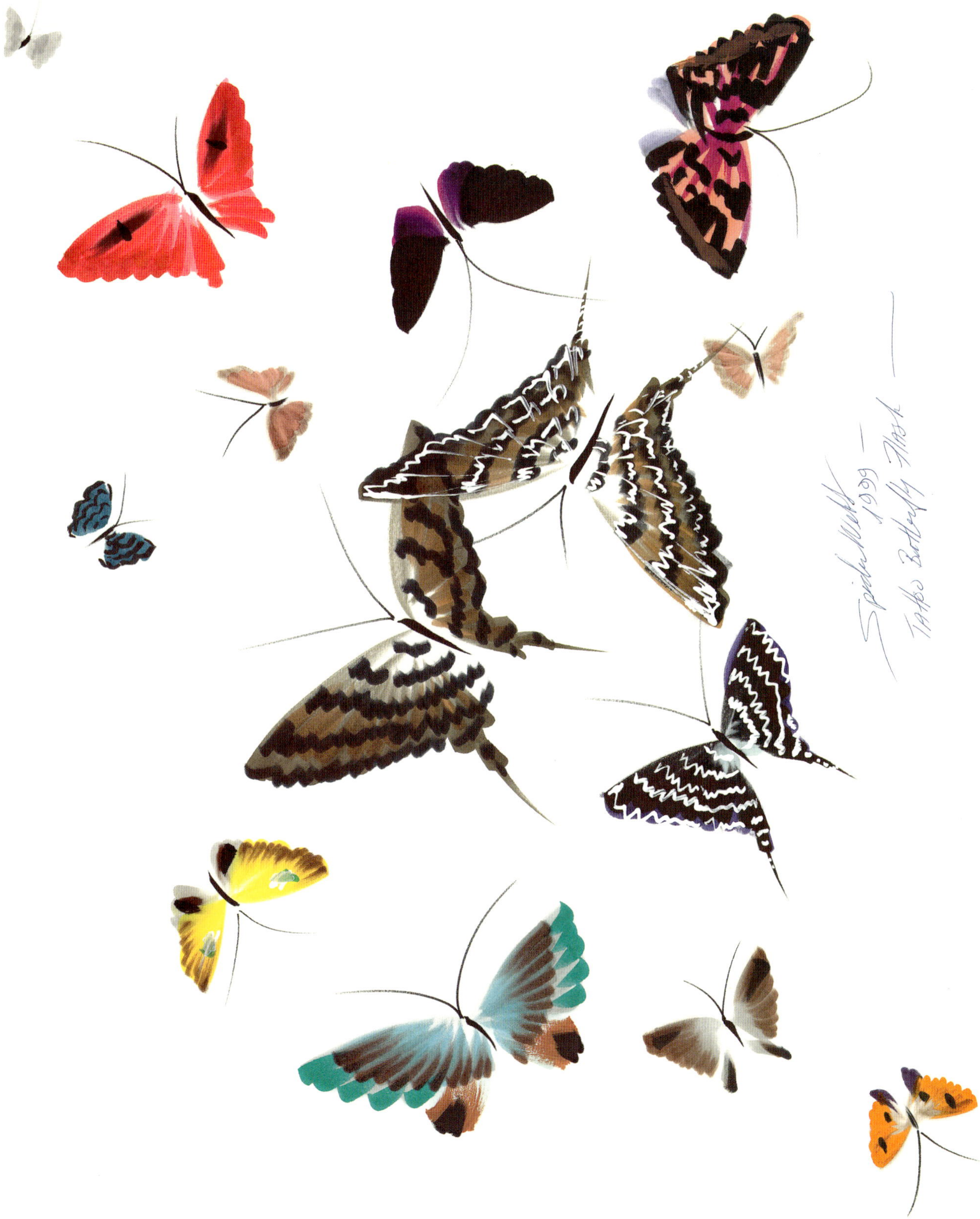
Spider Webb 1999 —
Tattoo Butterfly Flash

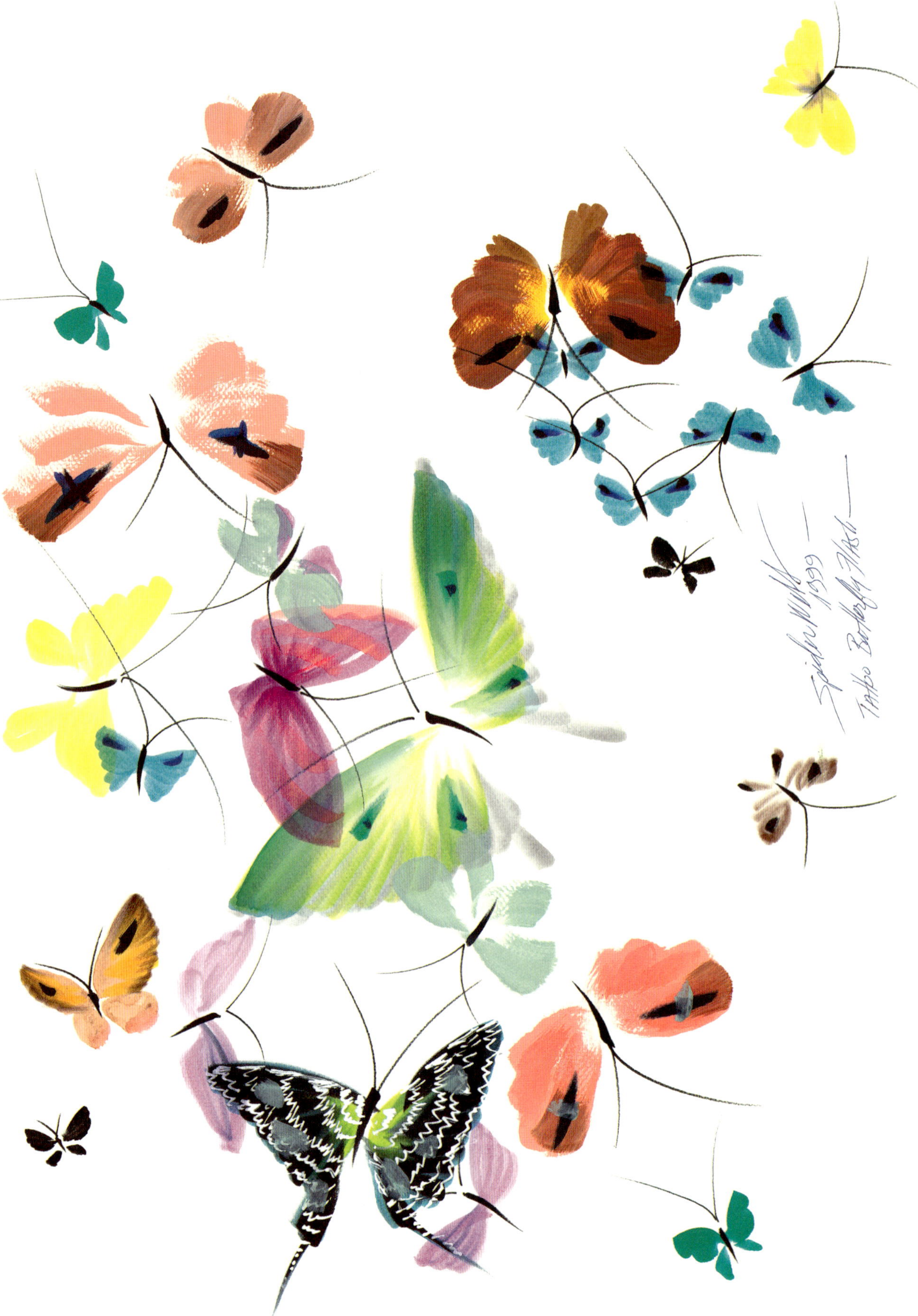
Spider Webb 1999
Tattoo Butterfly Flash

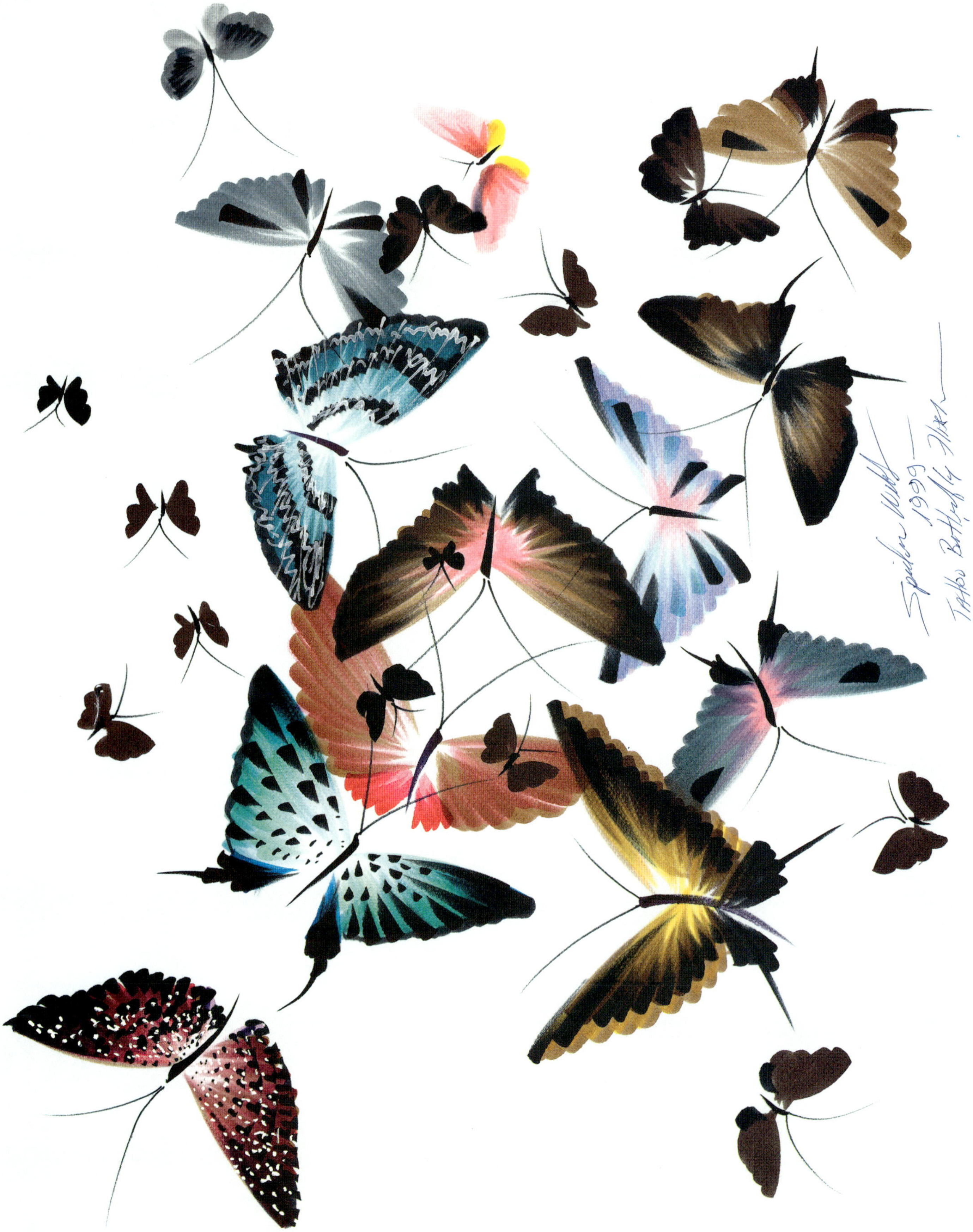

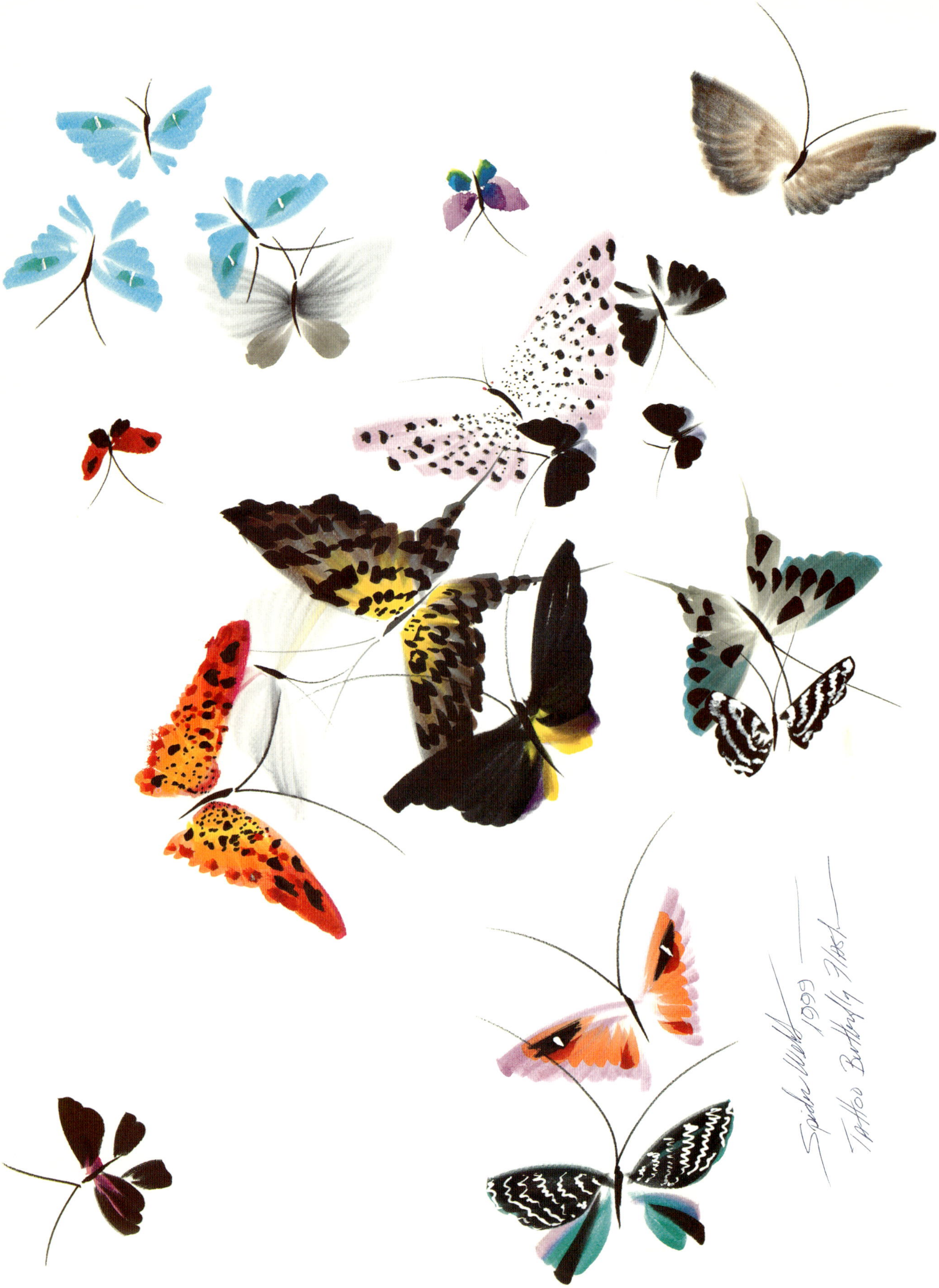
Spider Webb 1999
Tattoo Butterfly Flash

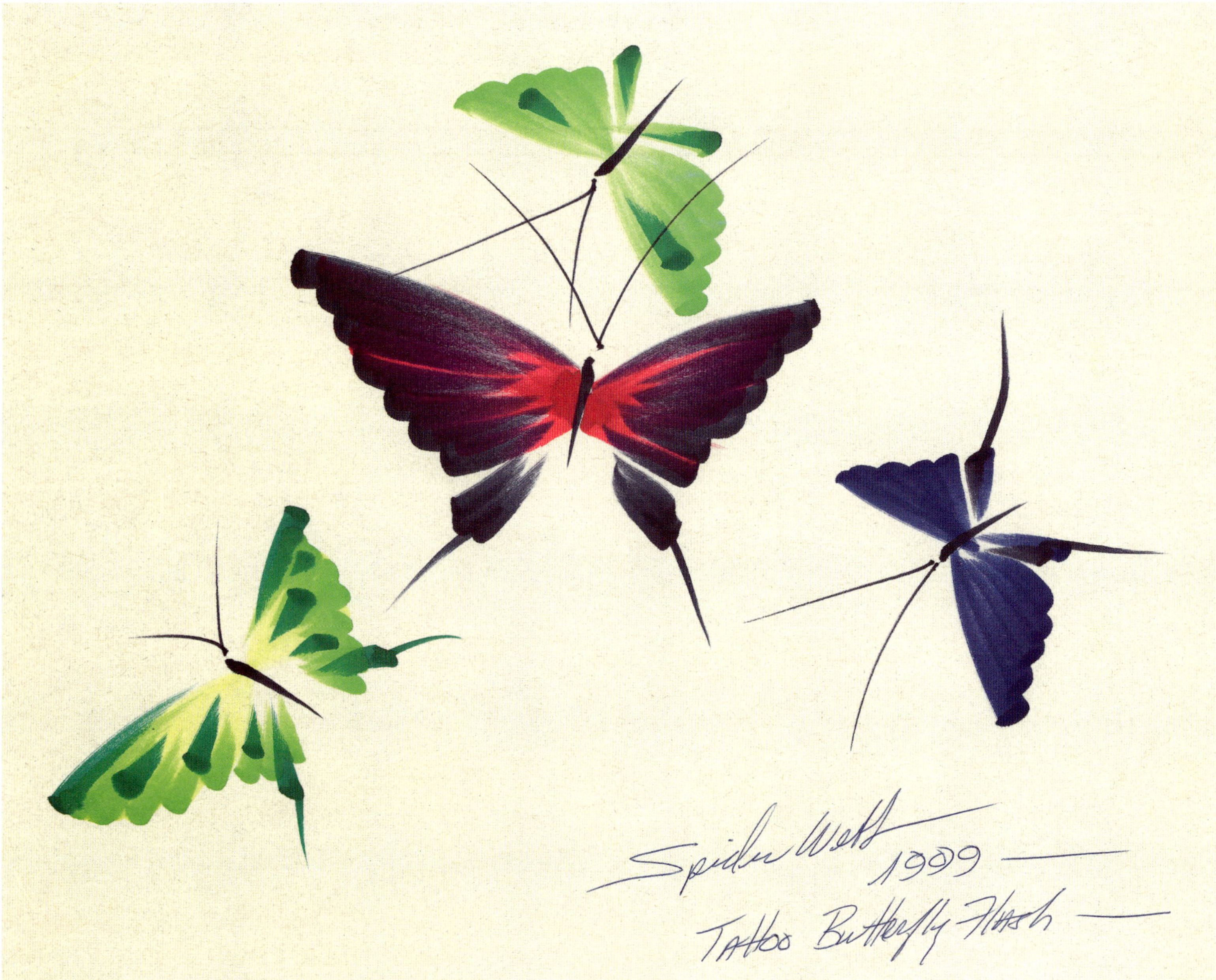
Spider Webb
1999
Tattoo Butterfly Flash

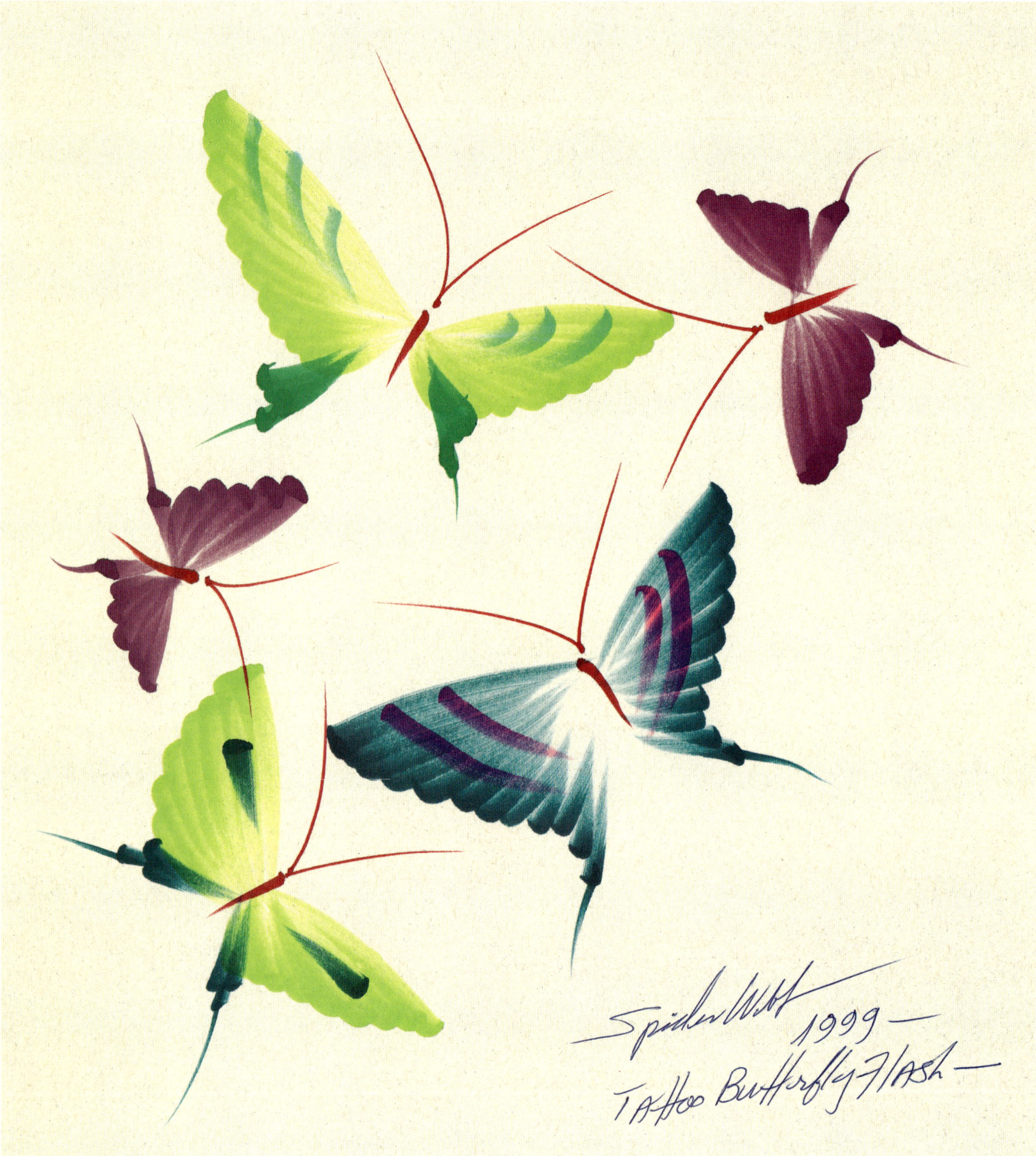

Spider Webb
1999 —
TAttoo Butterfly Flash —

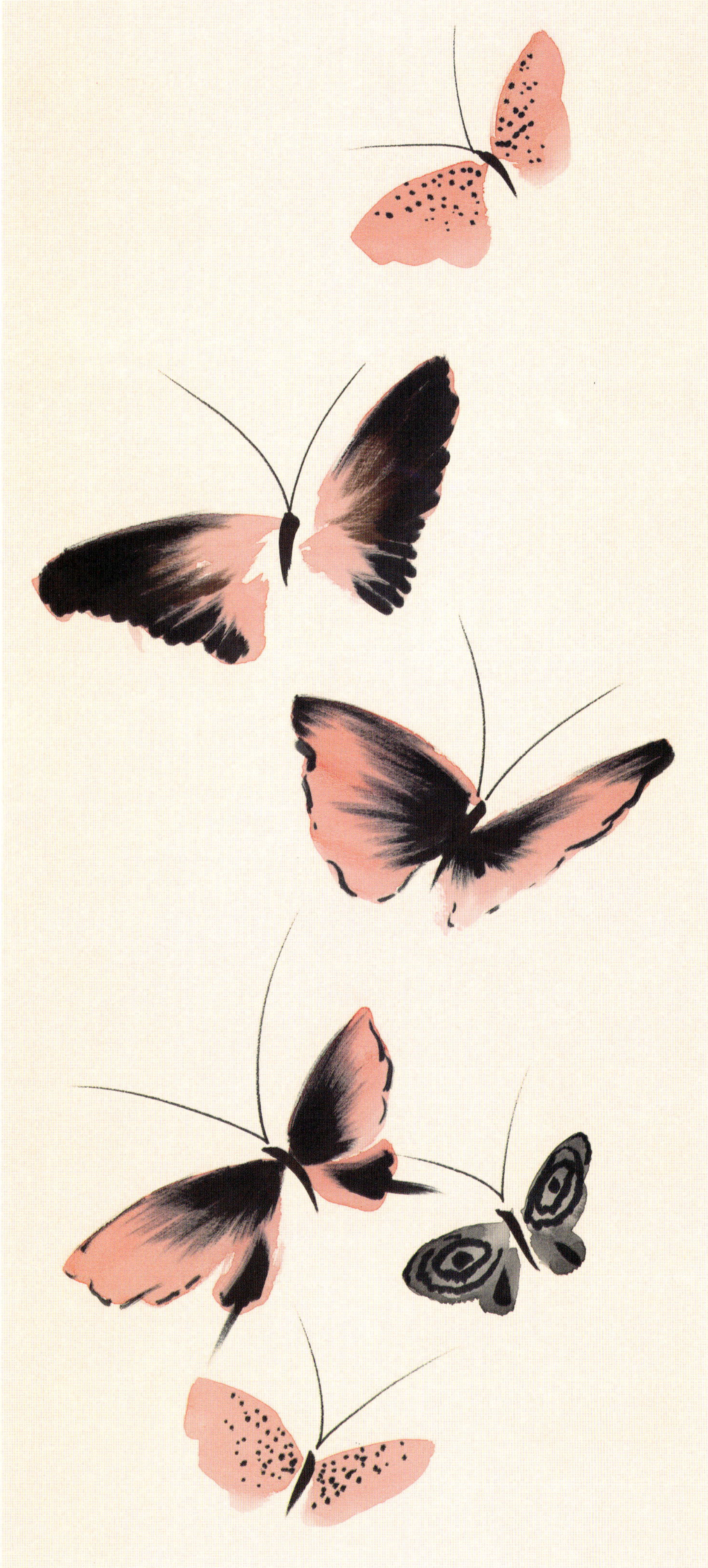

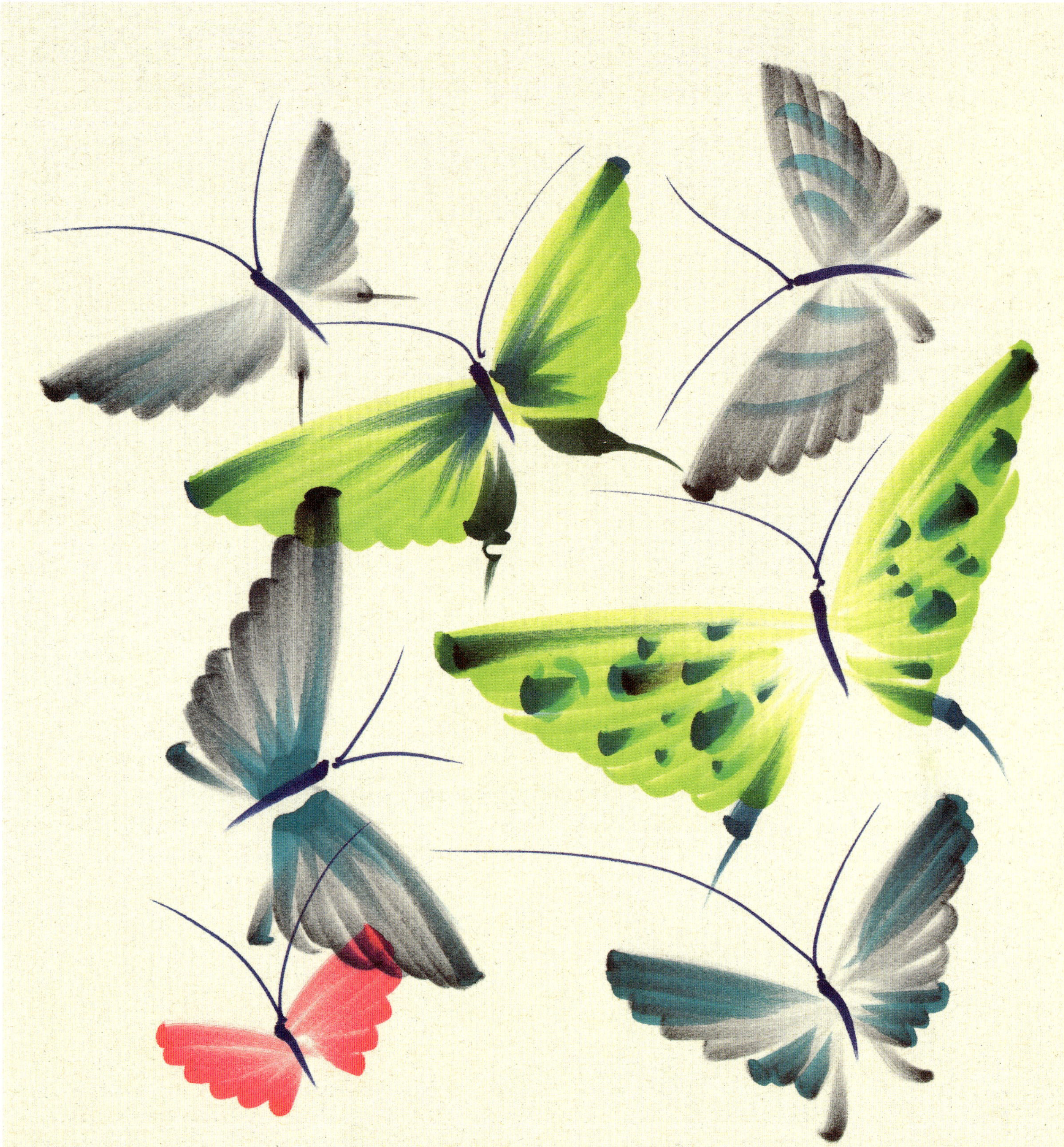

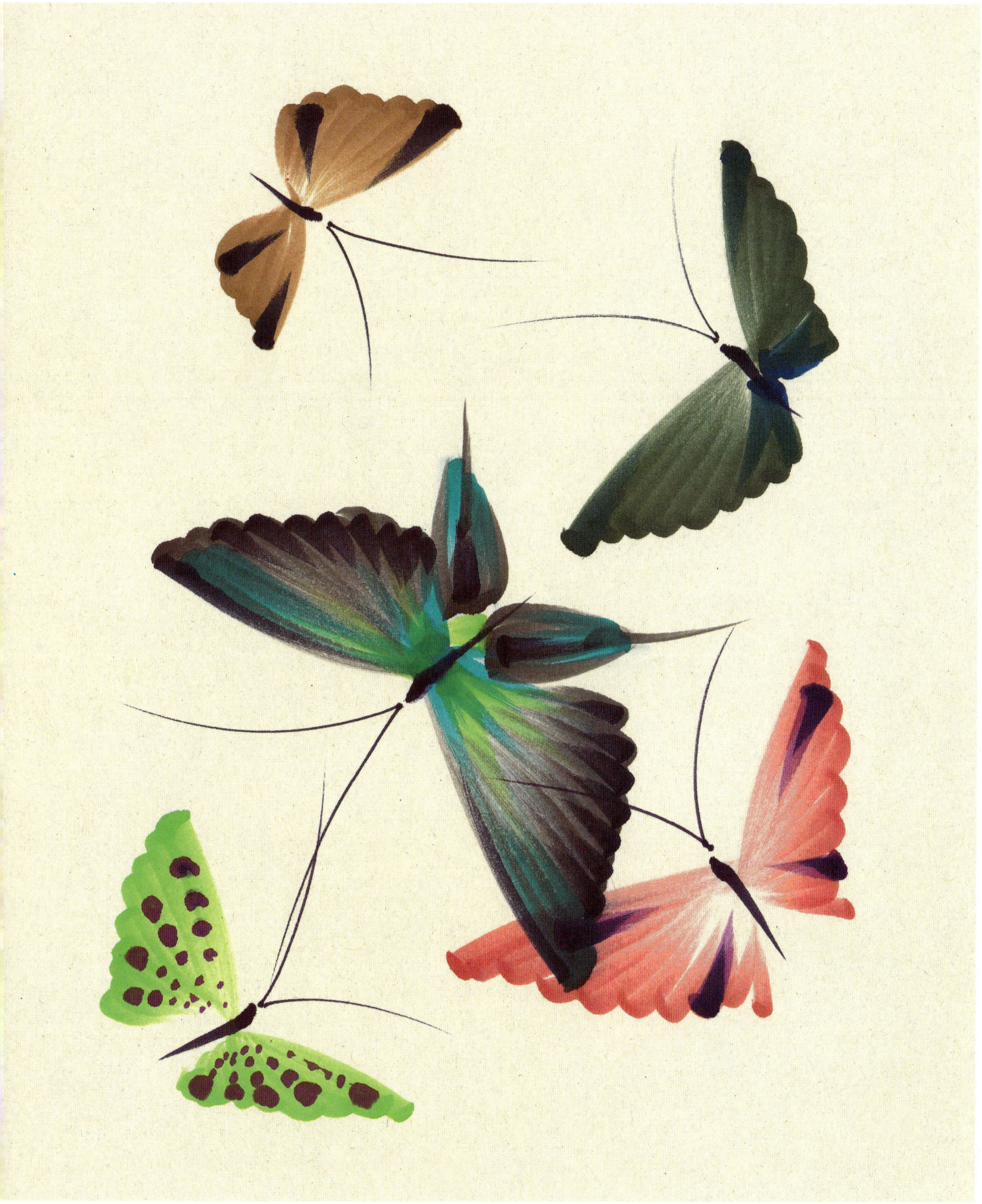

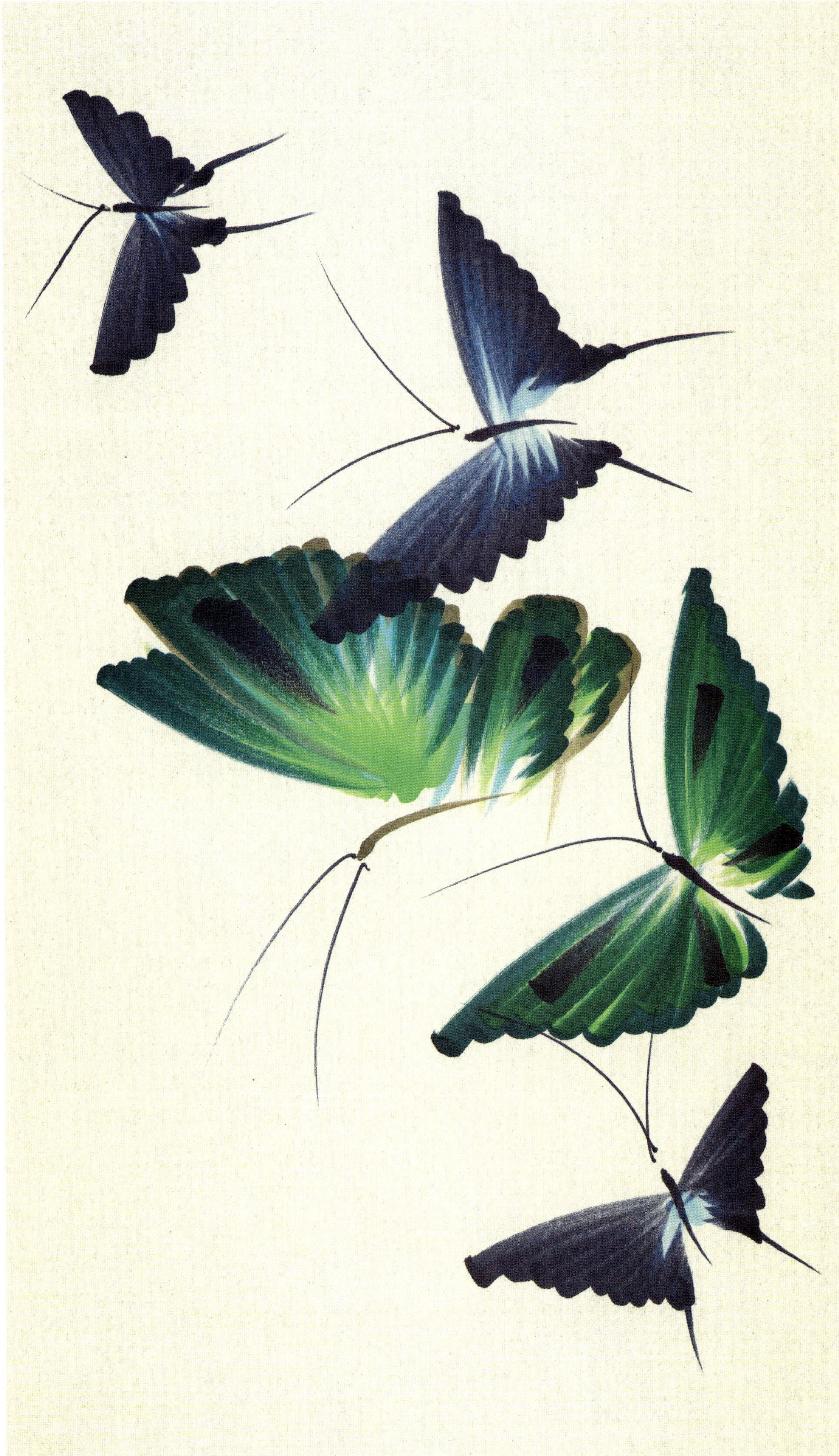

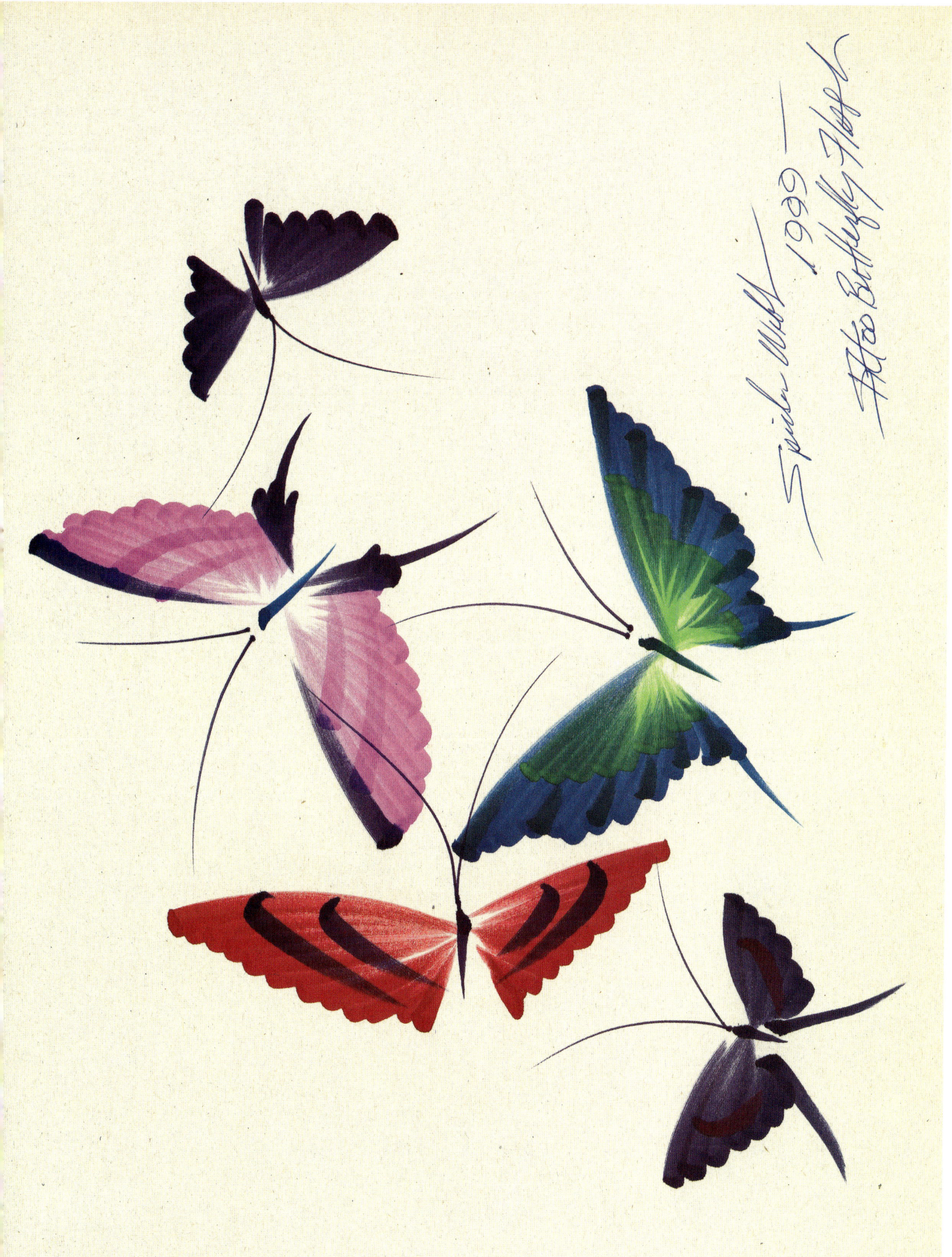

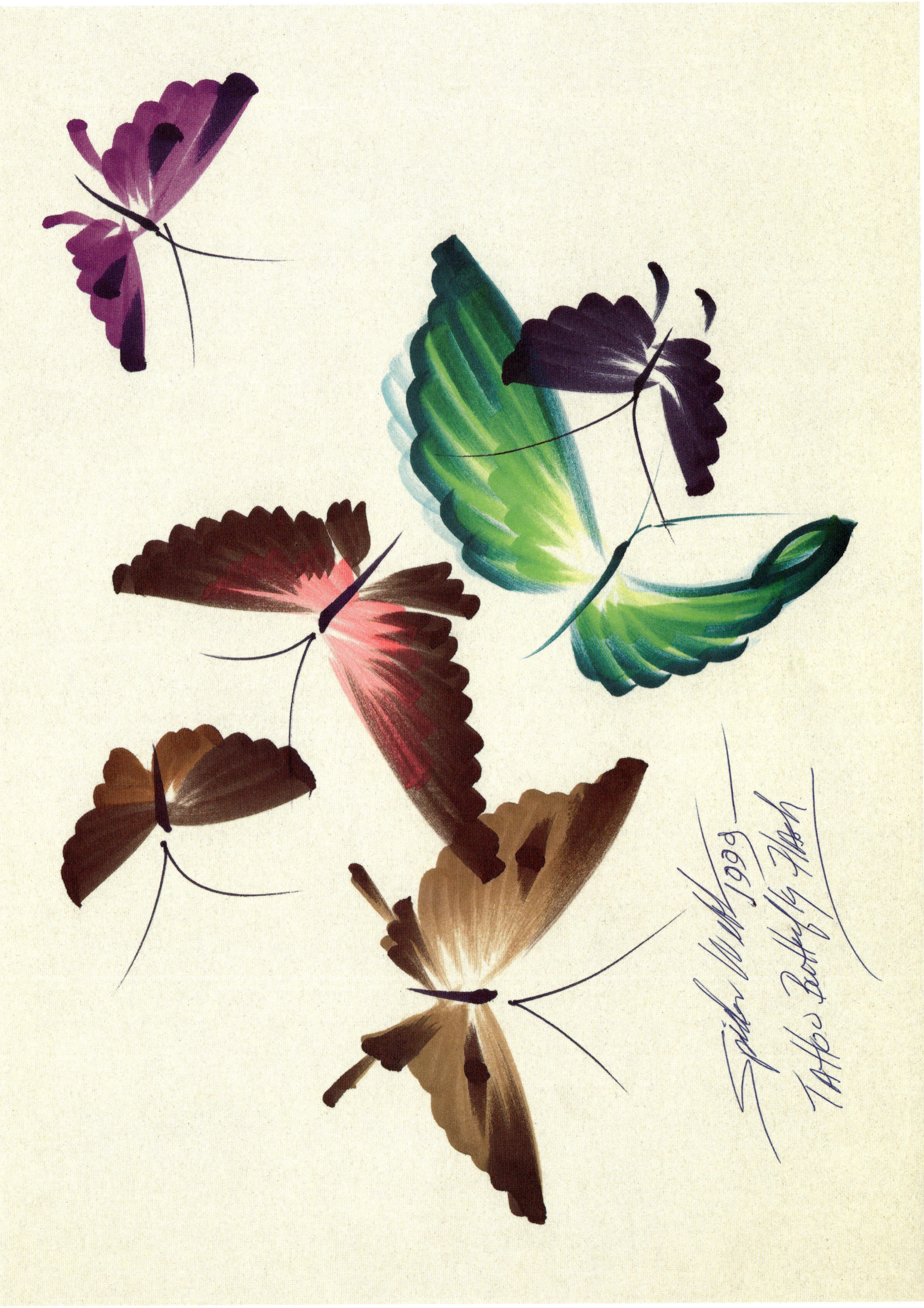
Spider Webb 1999
Tattoo Butterfly Flash

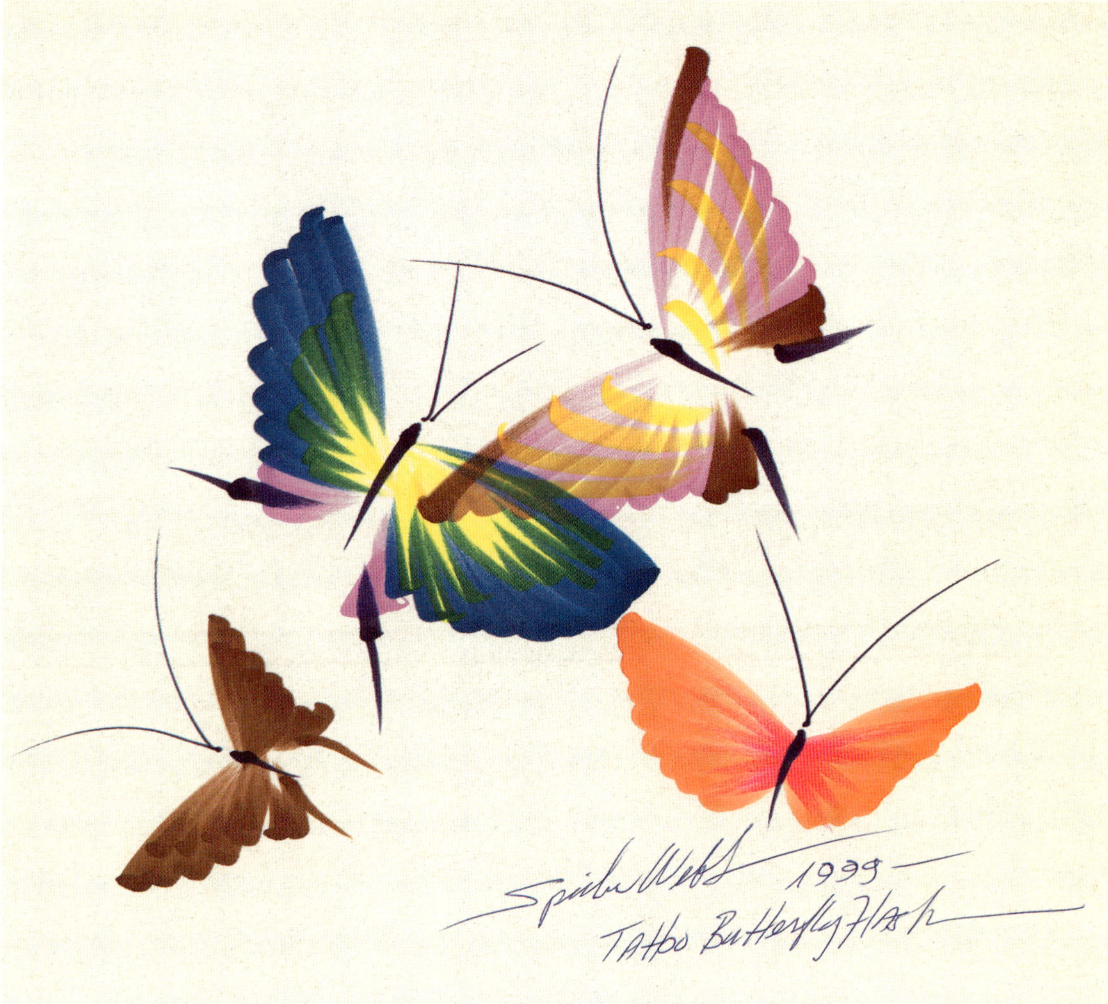
1999
TAttoo Butterfly Flash

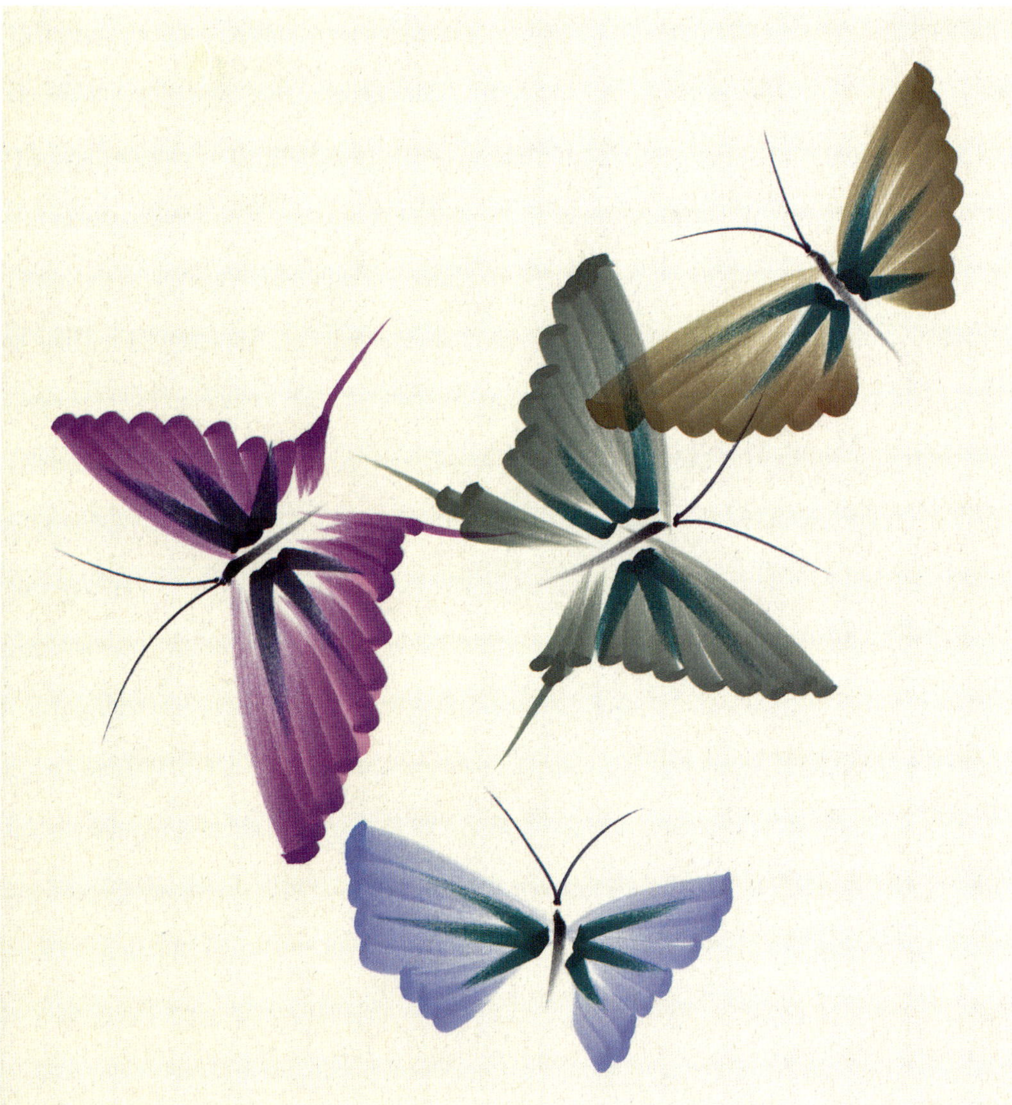

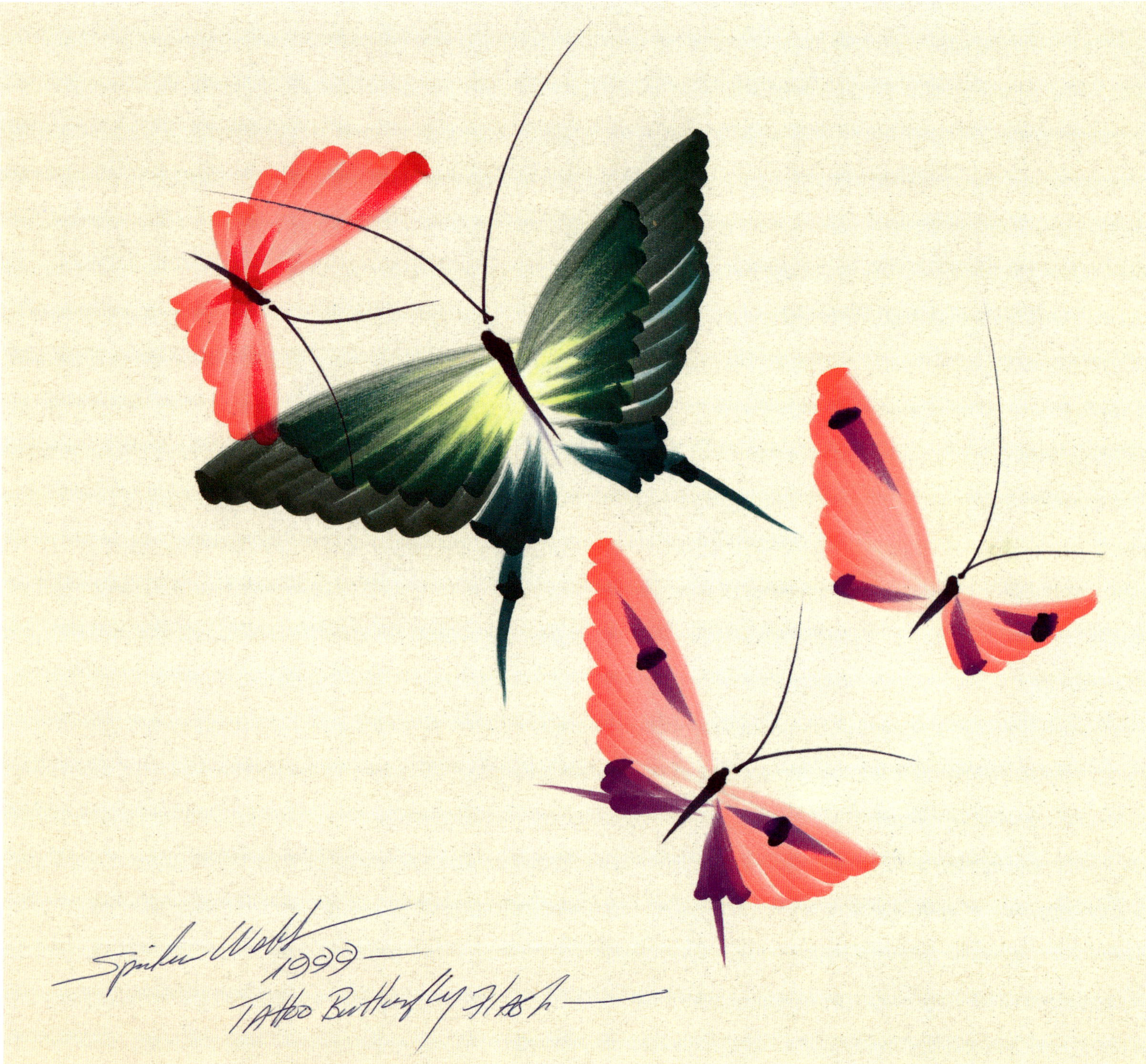
Spider Webb
1999
TAttoo Butterfly Flash

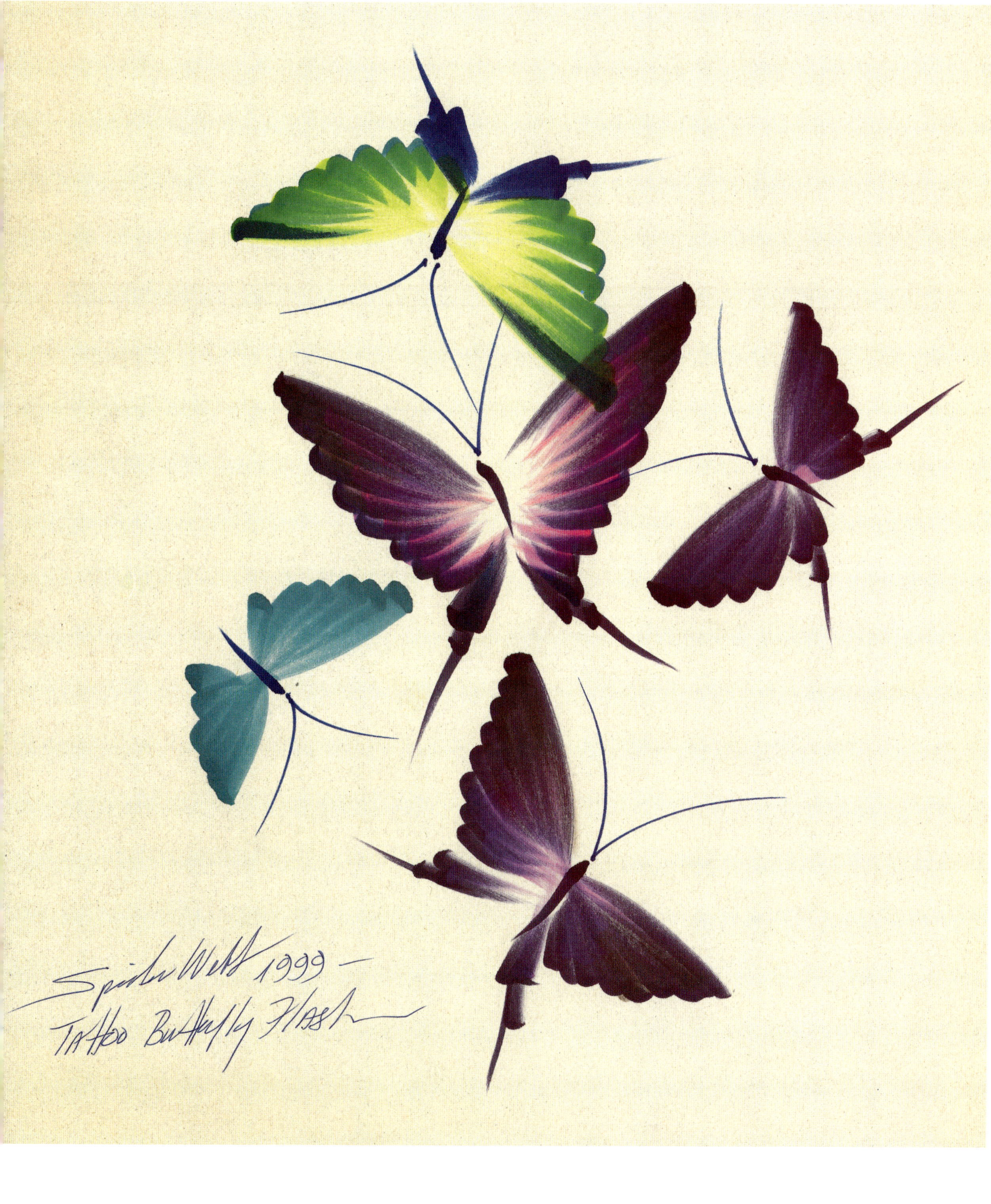
Spider Webb 1999 —
Tattoo Butterfly Flash

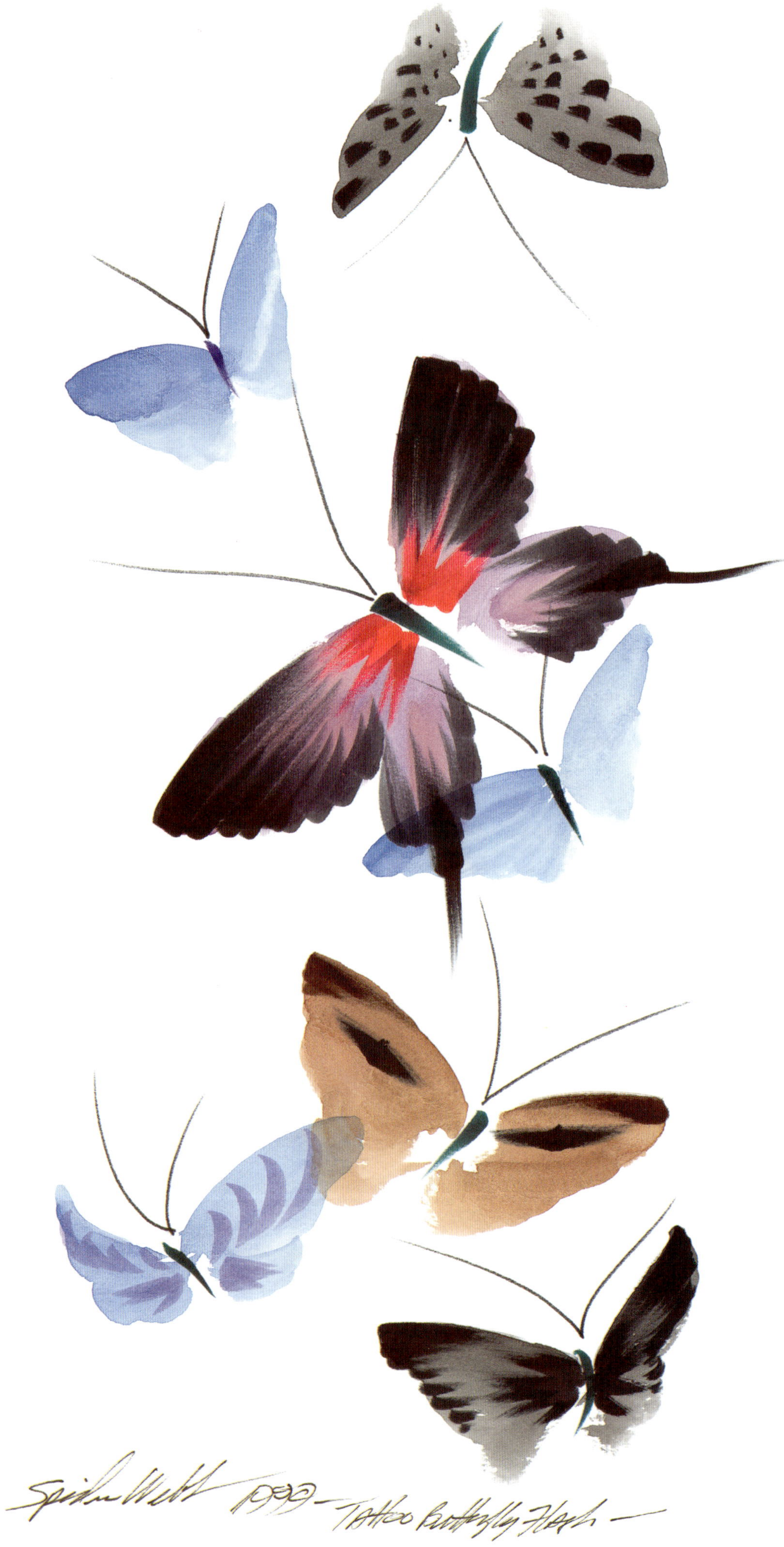

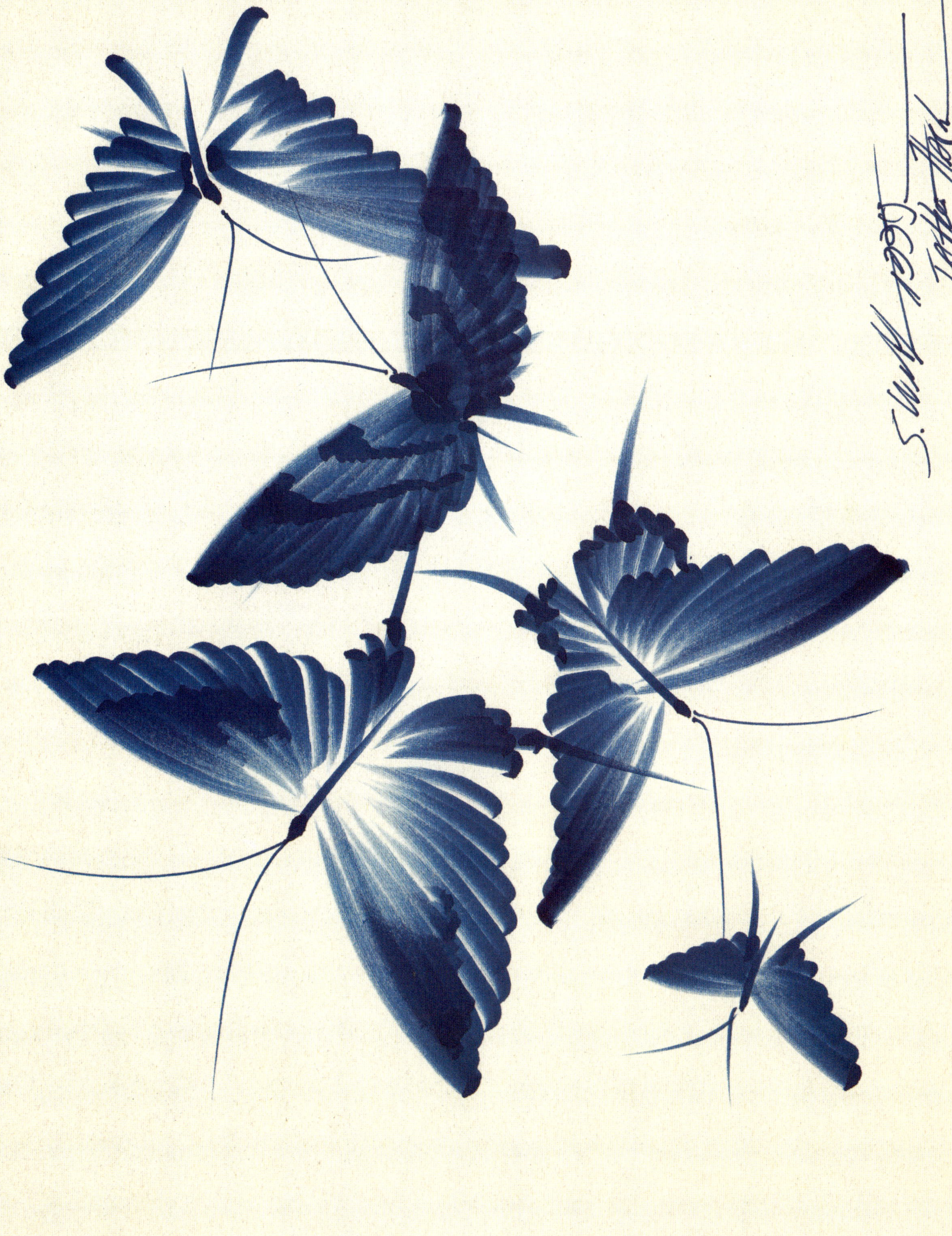

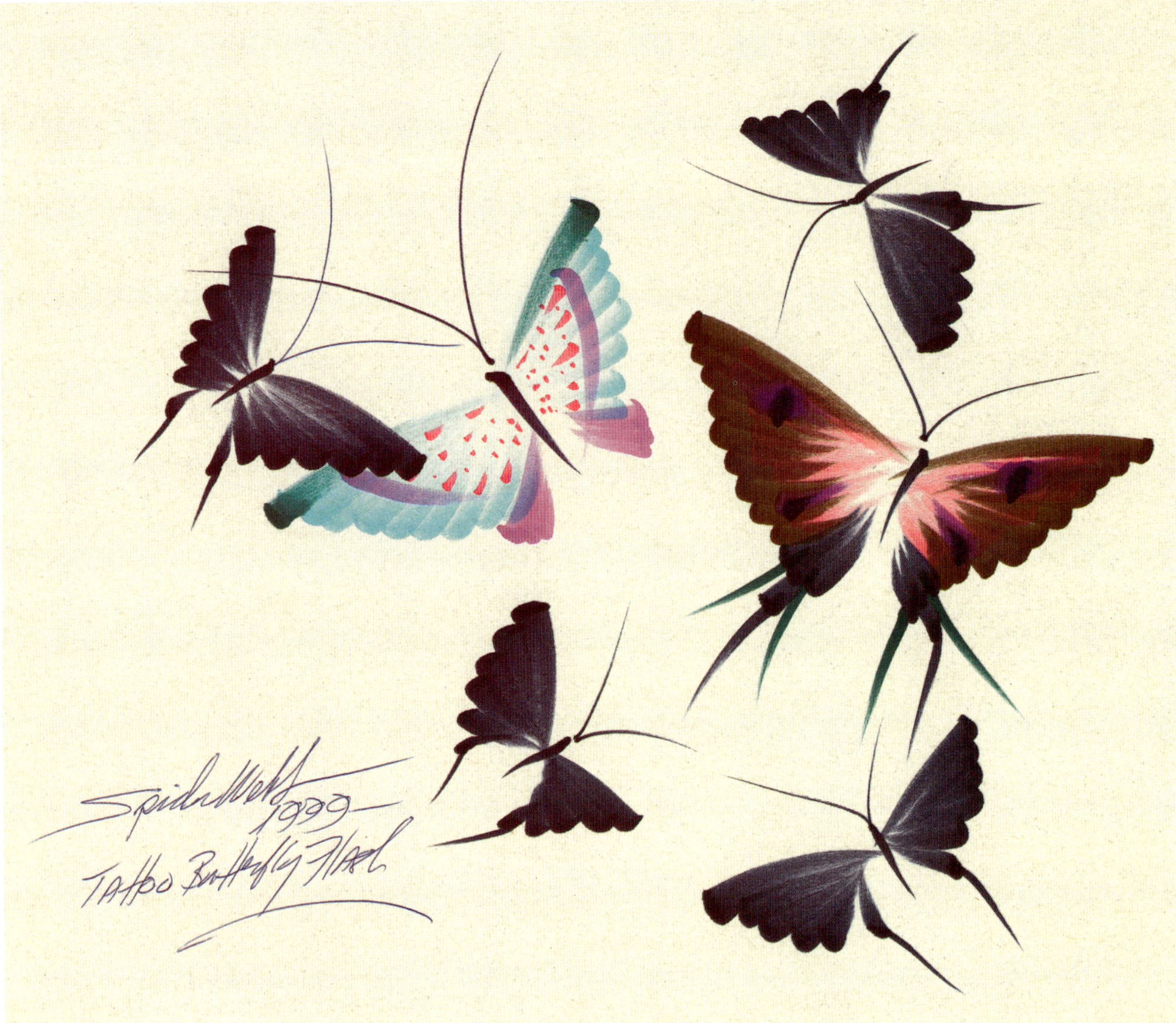
Spider Webb
1999
TAttoo Butterfly Flash

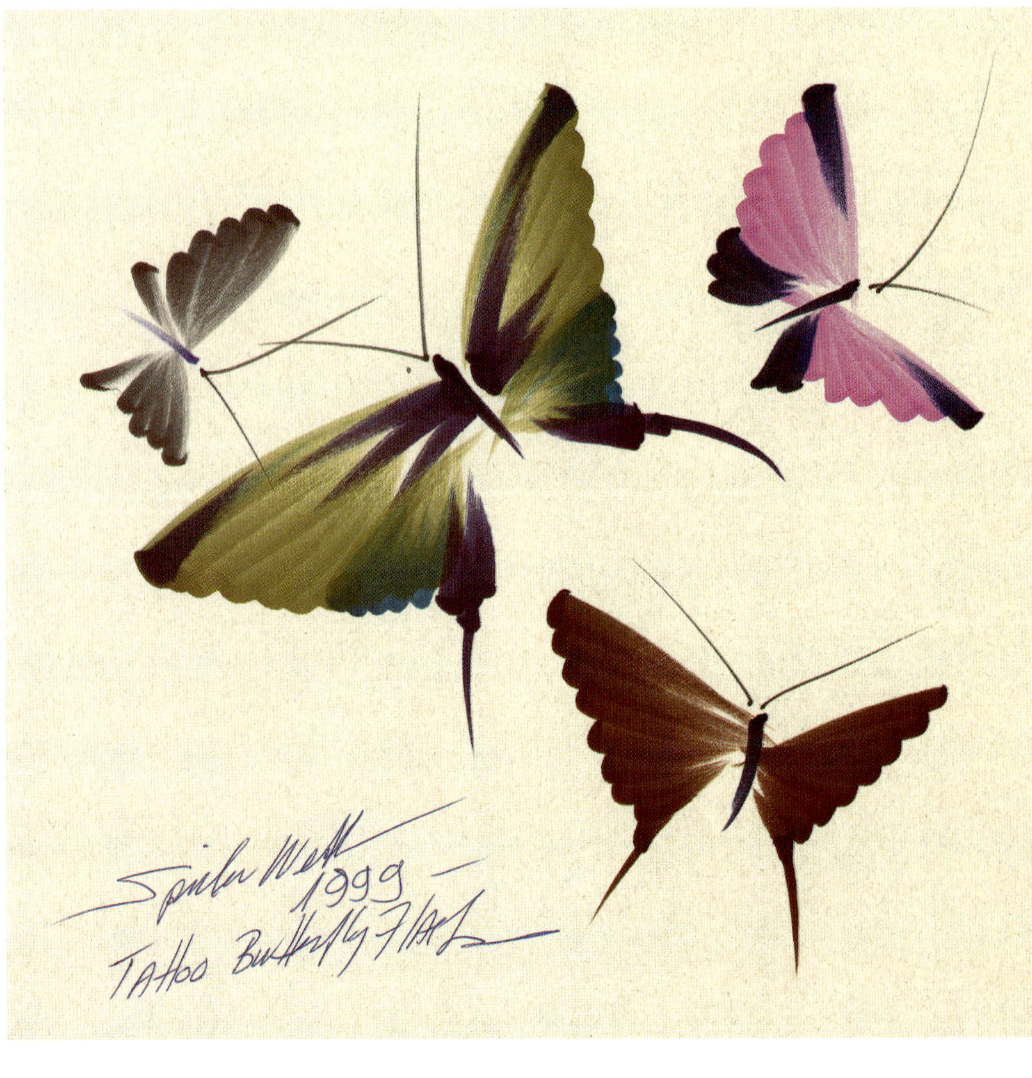
Spider Webb
1999
TAttoo Butterfly Flash

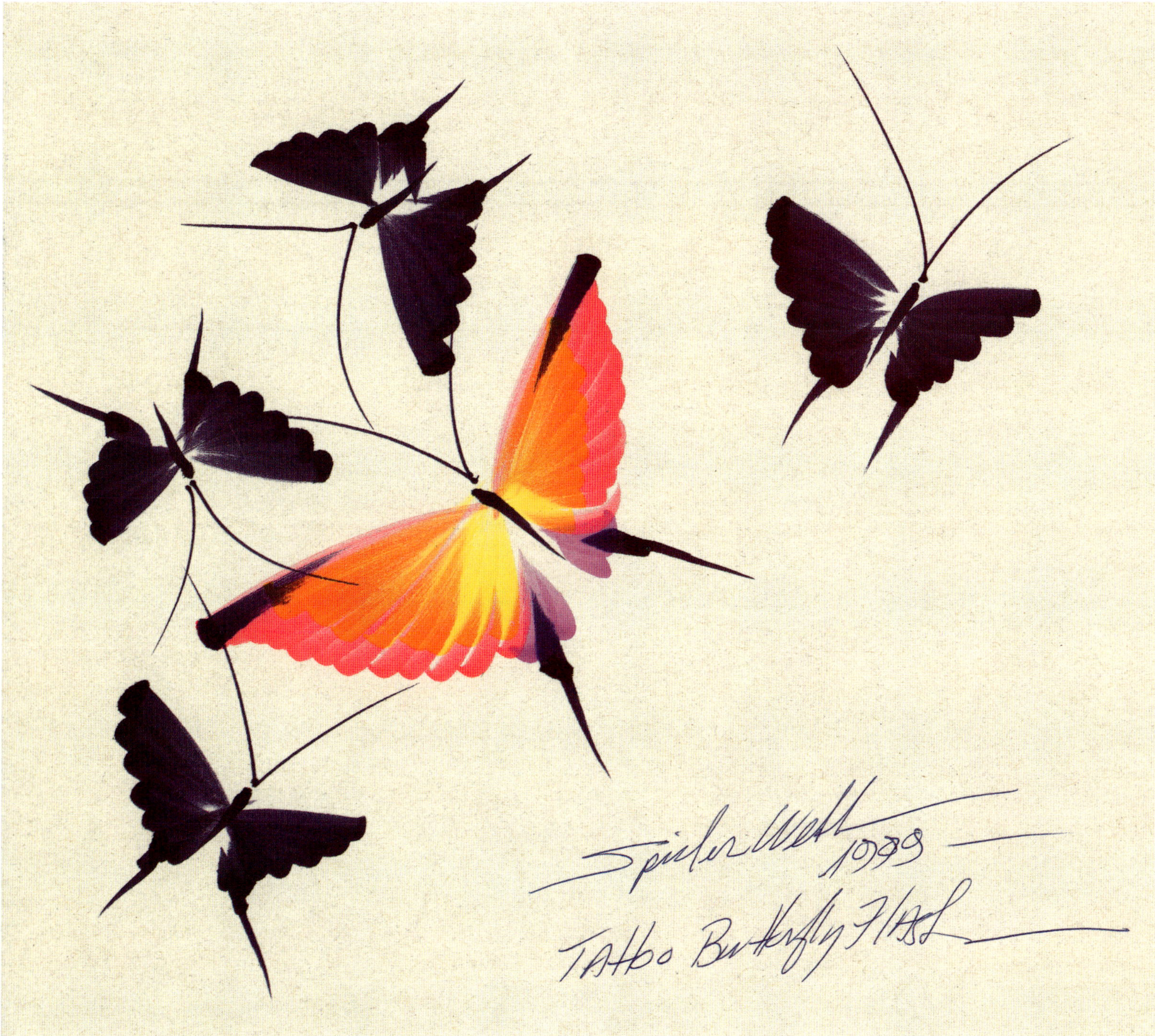
Spider Webb
TAttoo Butterfly Flash

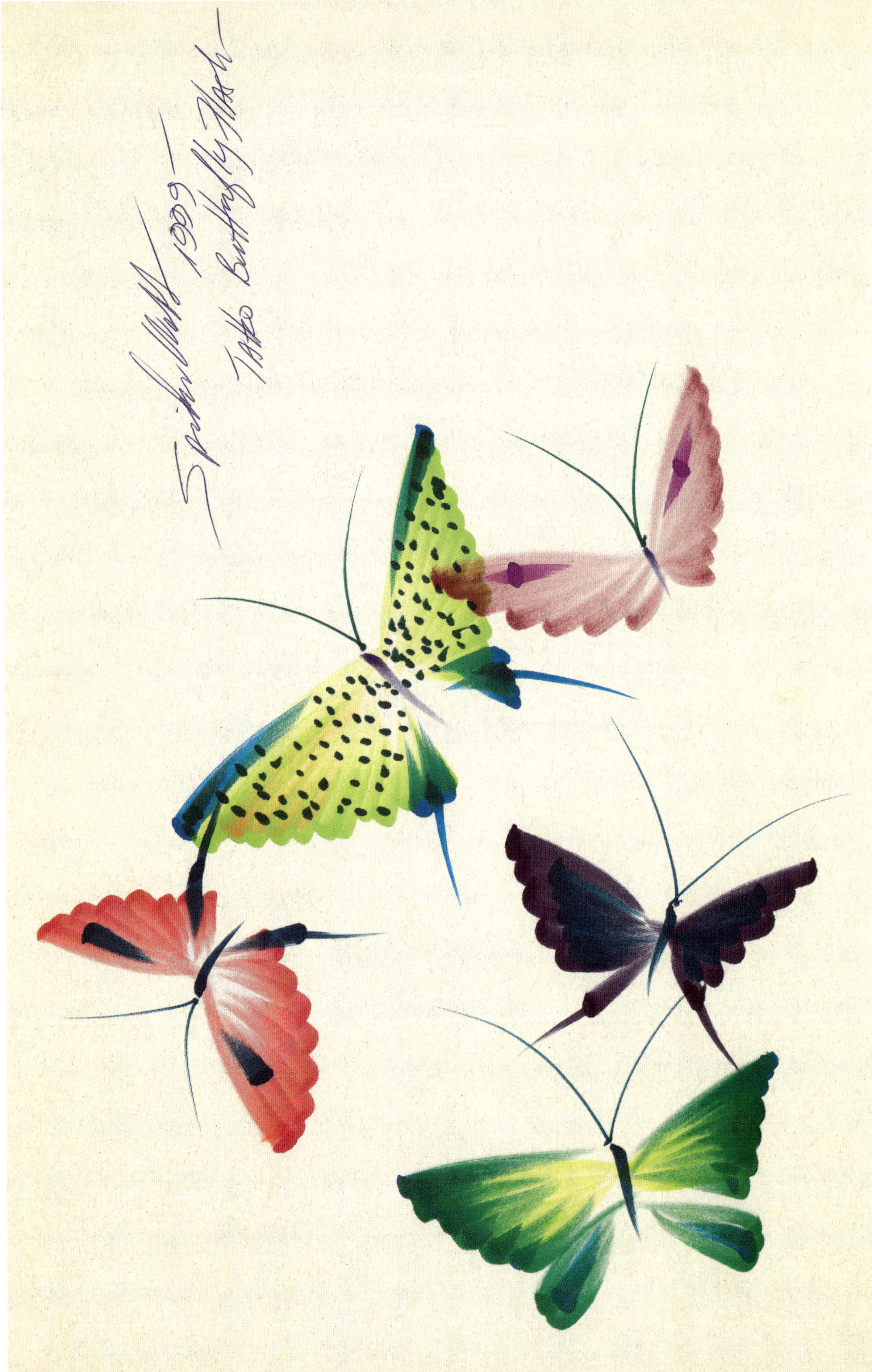

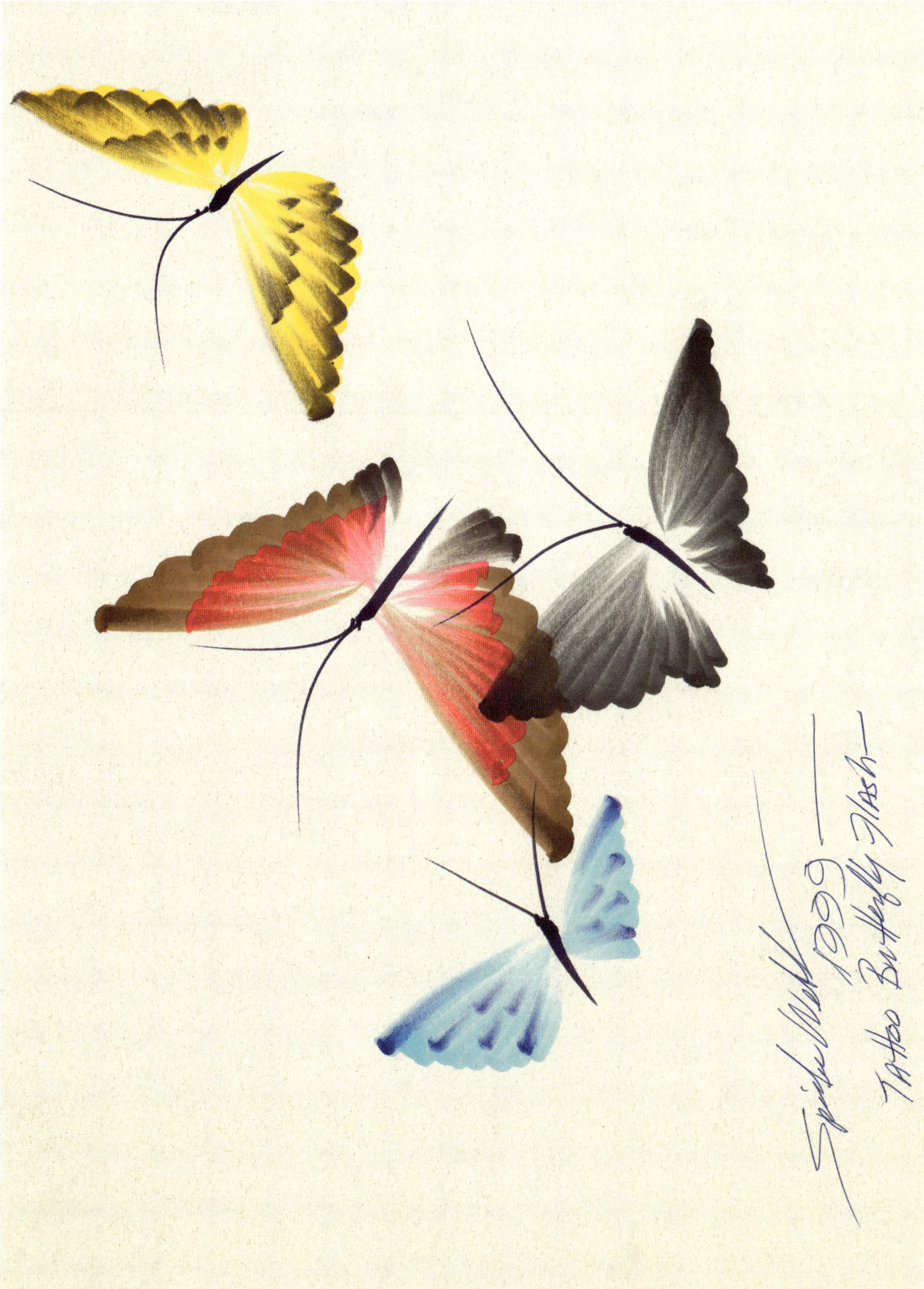
1999
Tattoo Butterfly Flash

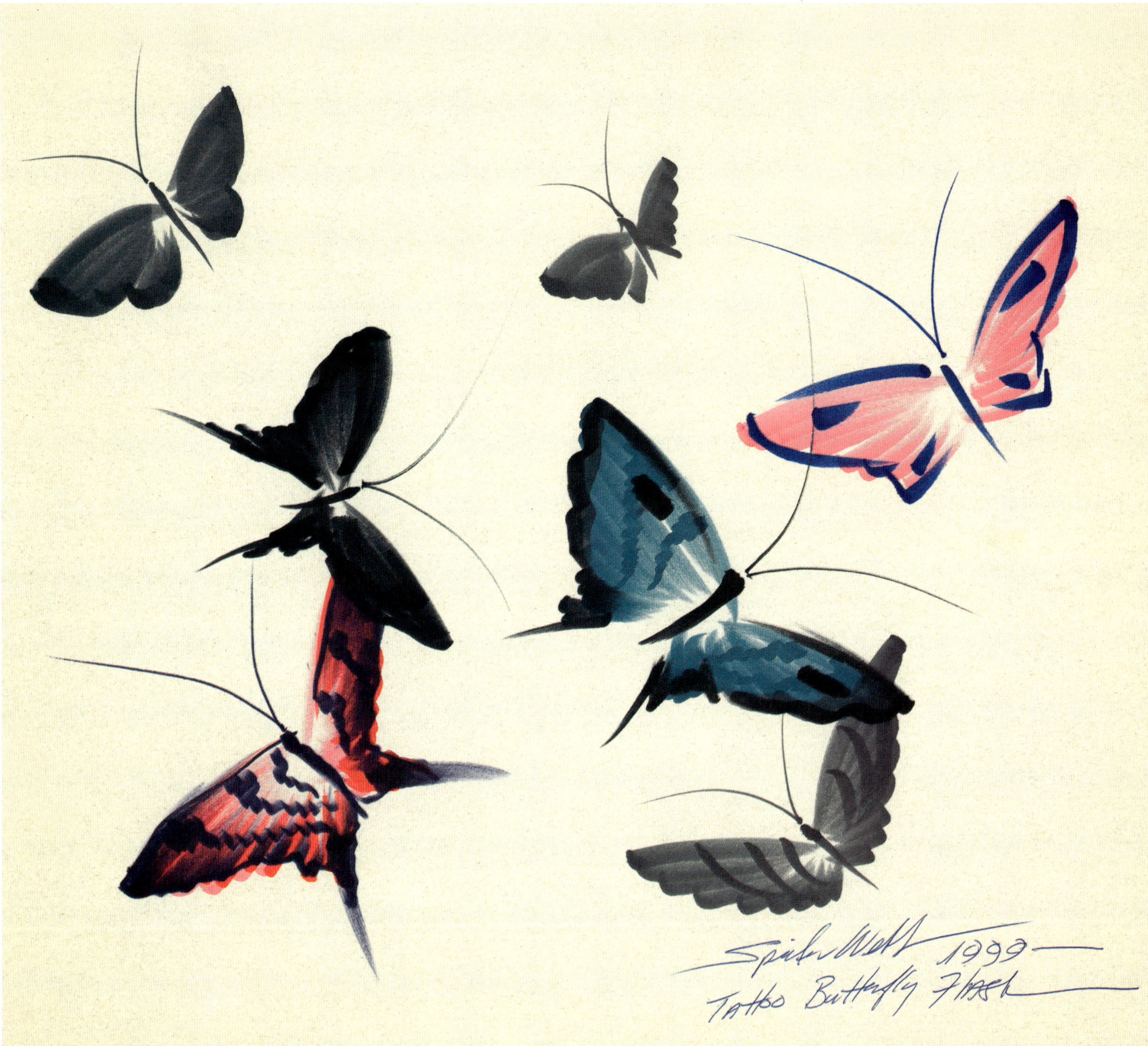
Spider Webb 1999
Tattoo Butterfly Flash

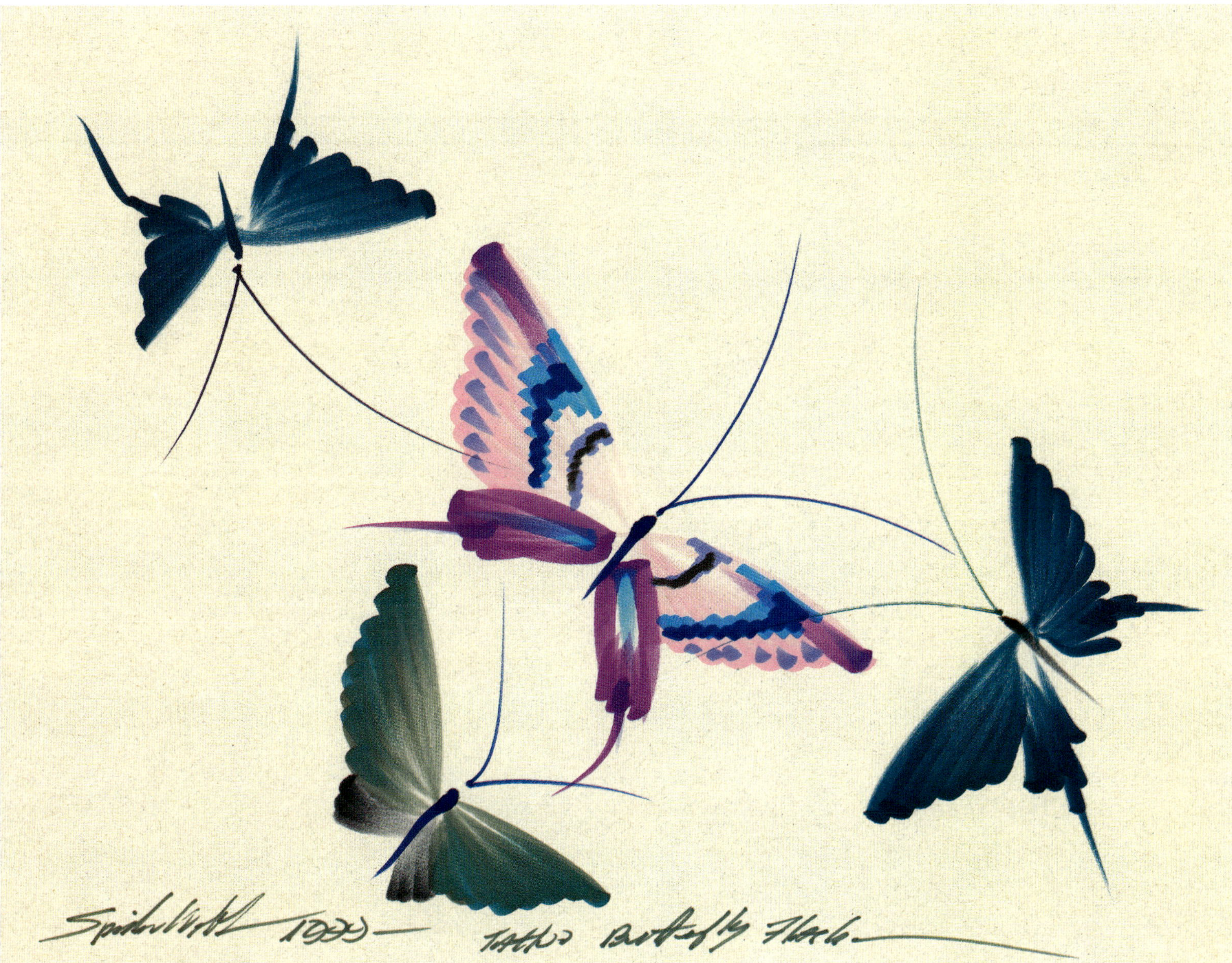

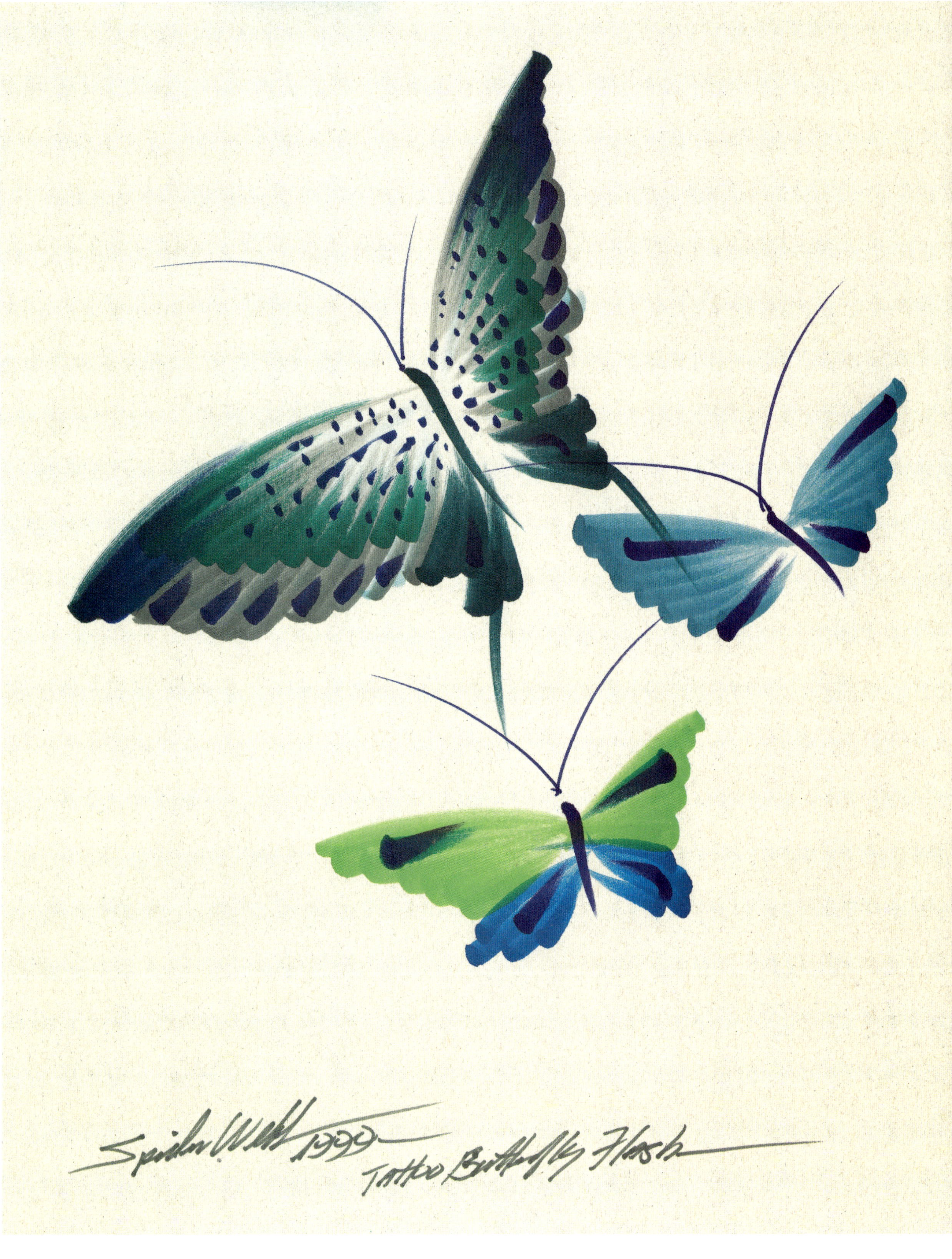
Spider Webb 1990
Tattoo Butterfly Flash

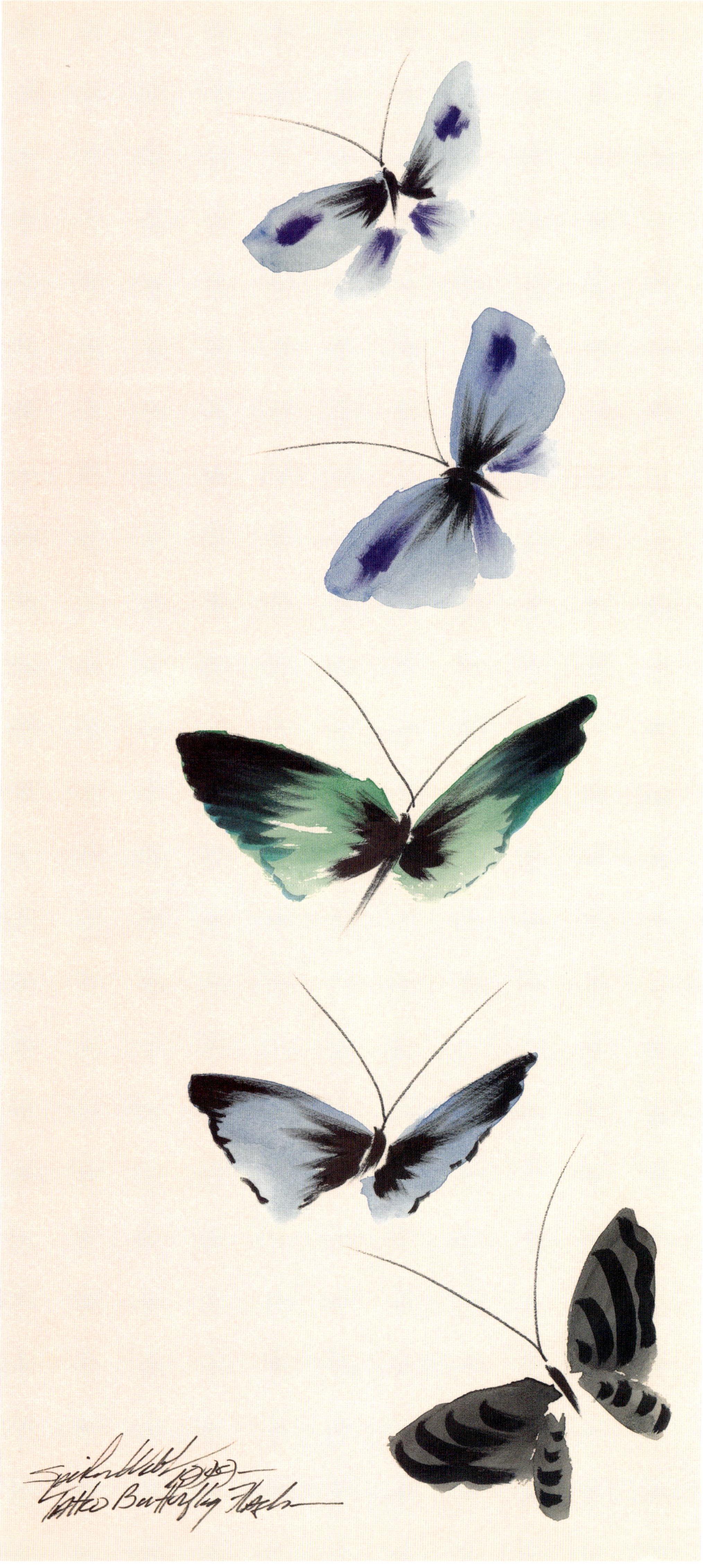

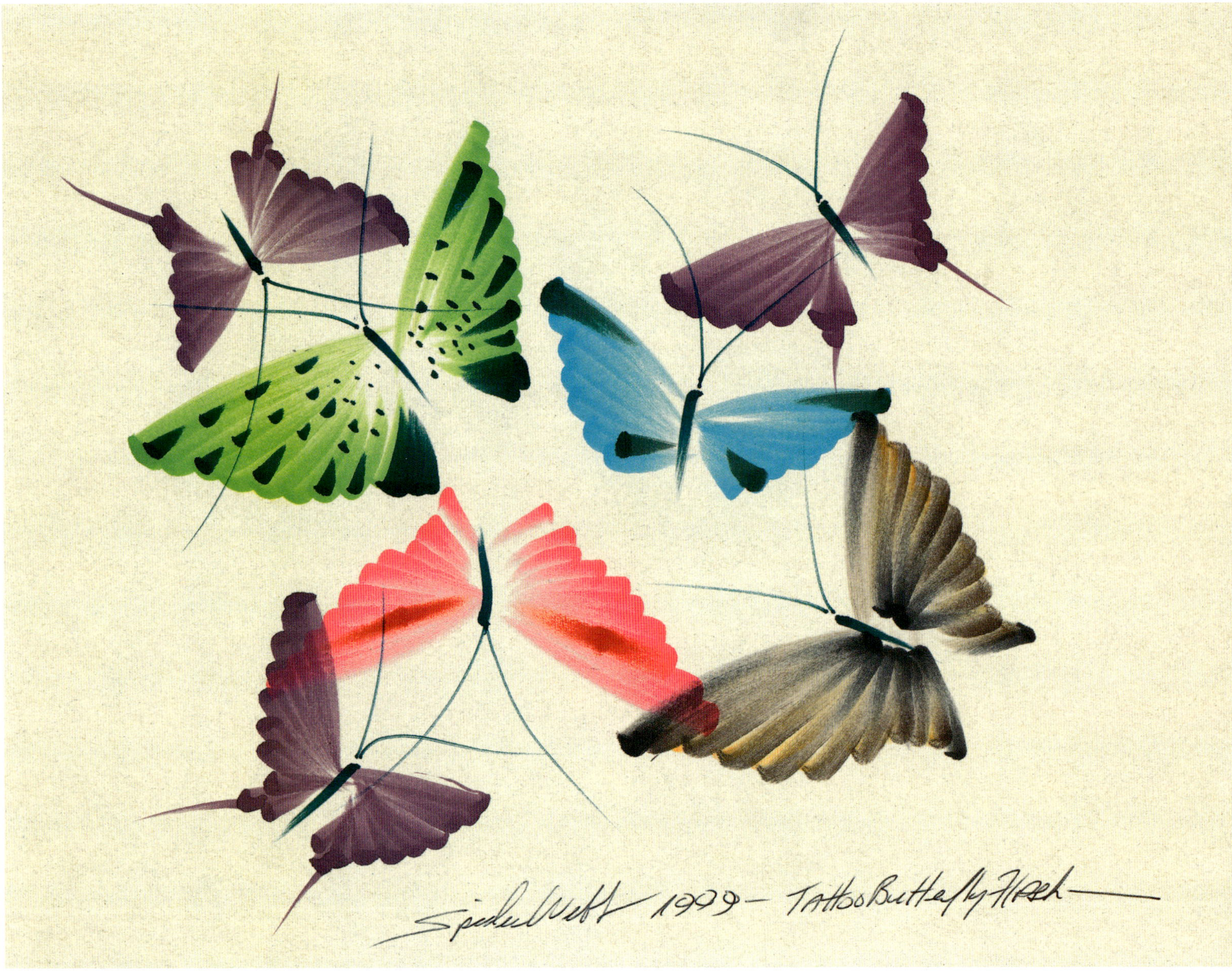
SpiderWebb 1999 - TattooButterflyFlash

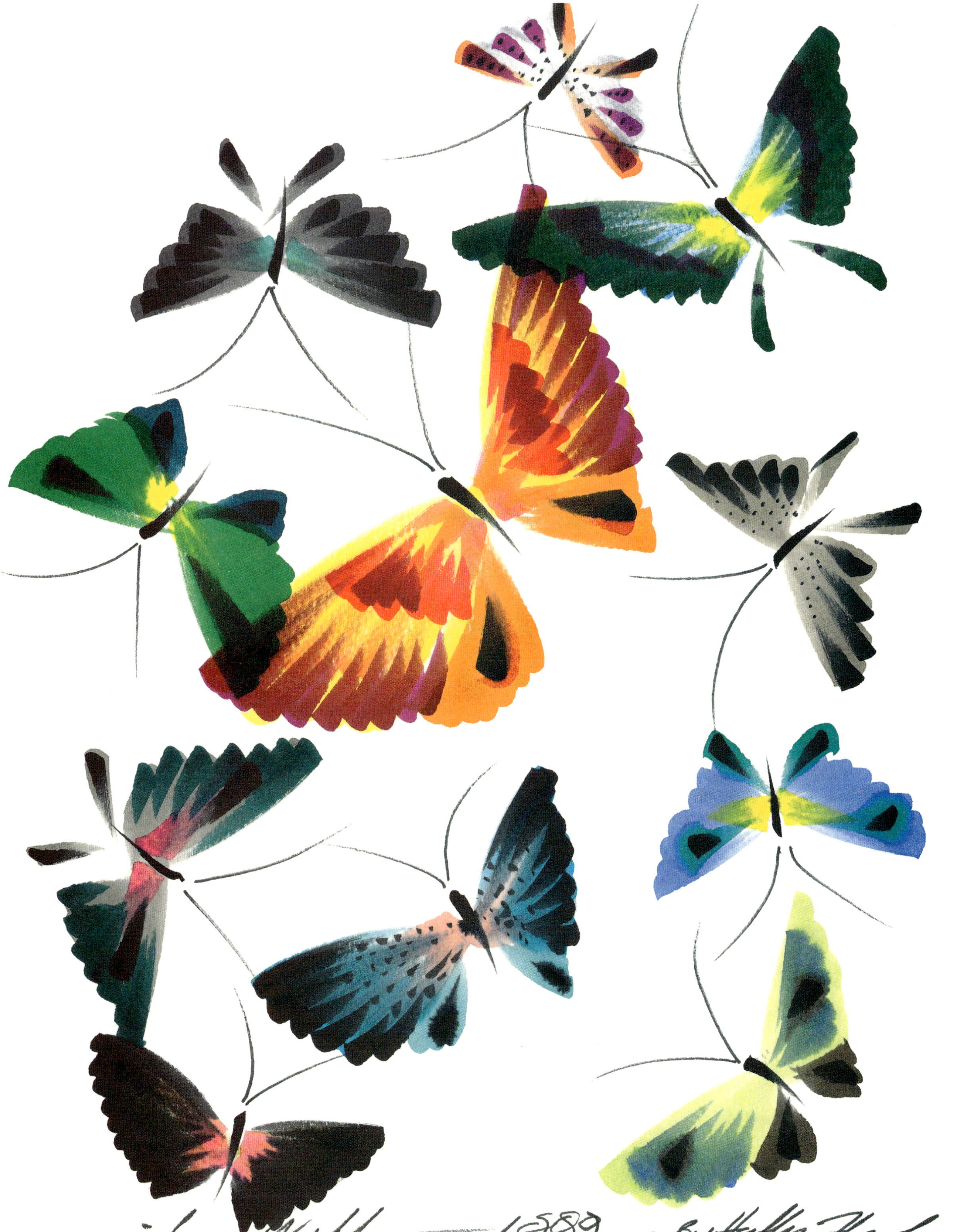
1989

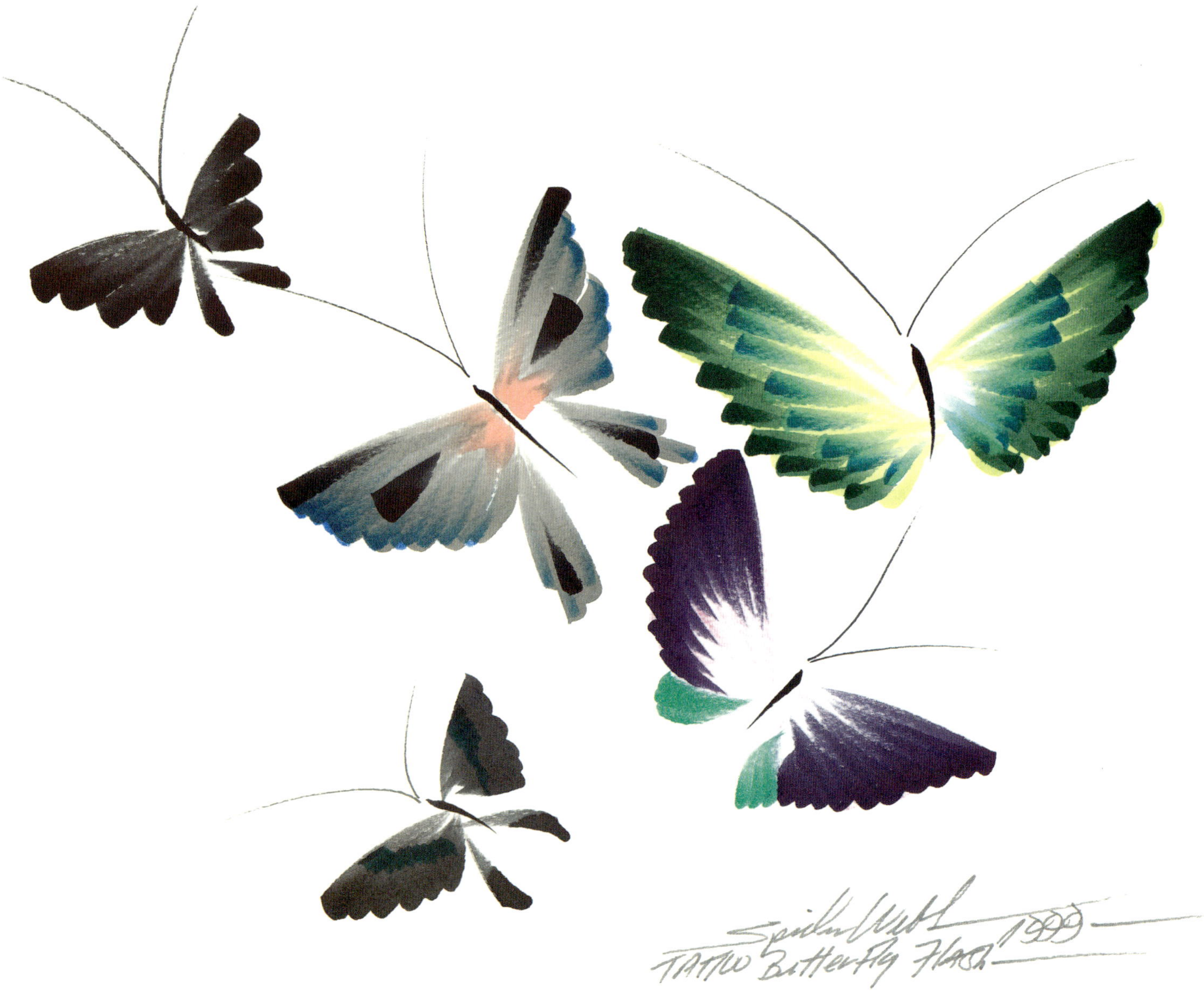
TATTOO Butterfly Flash

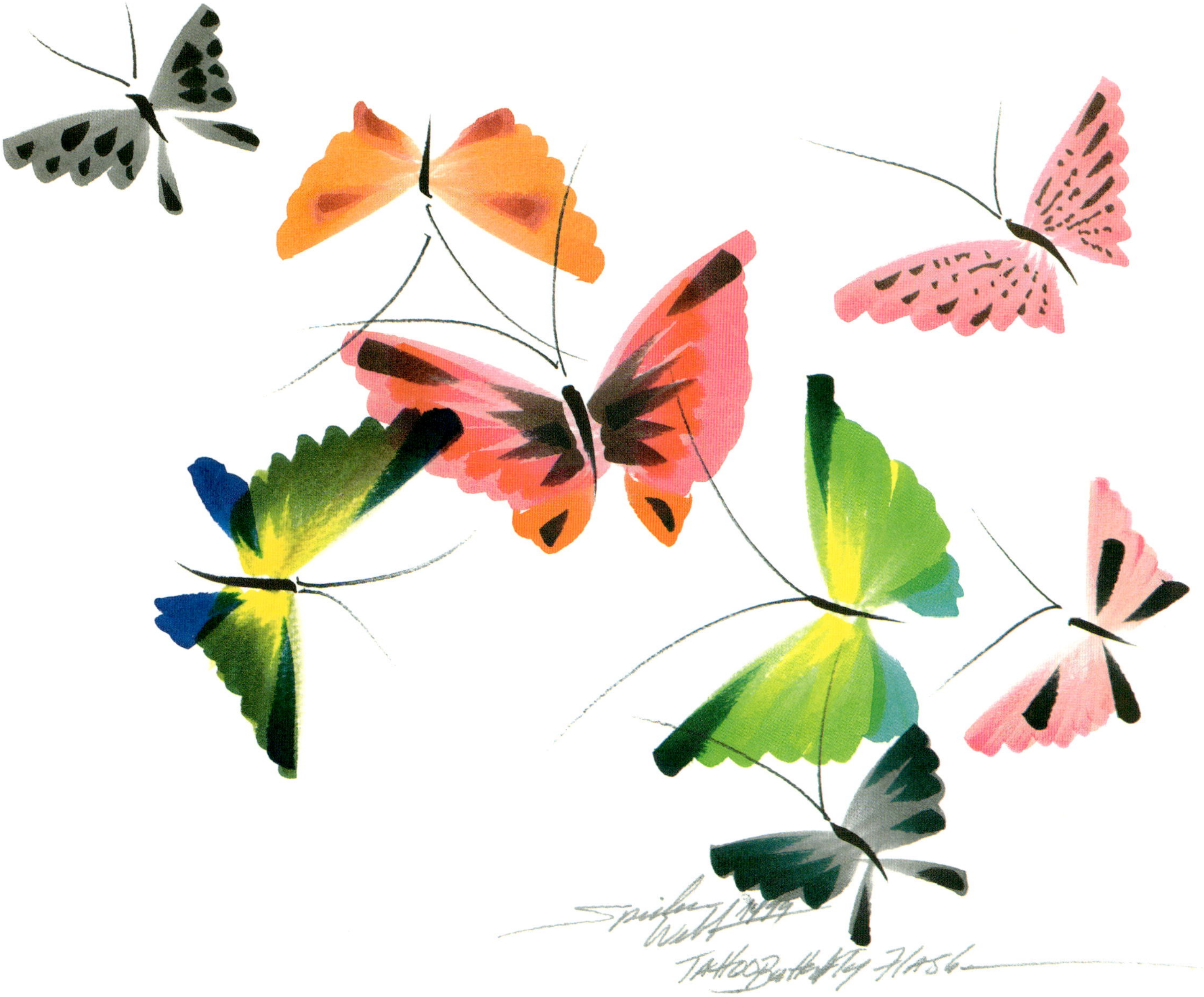

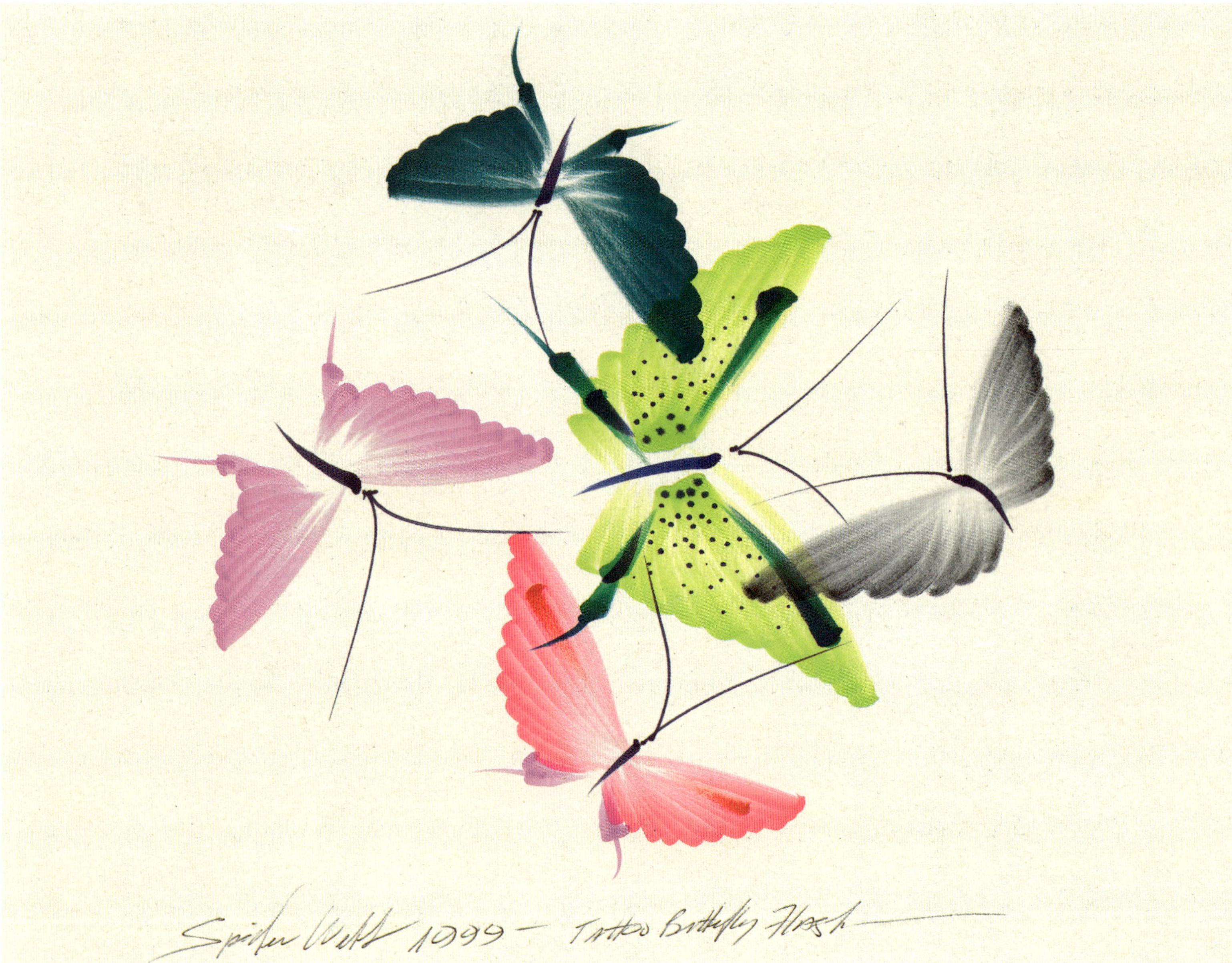
Spider Webb 1999 – Tattoo Butterfly Flash

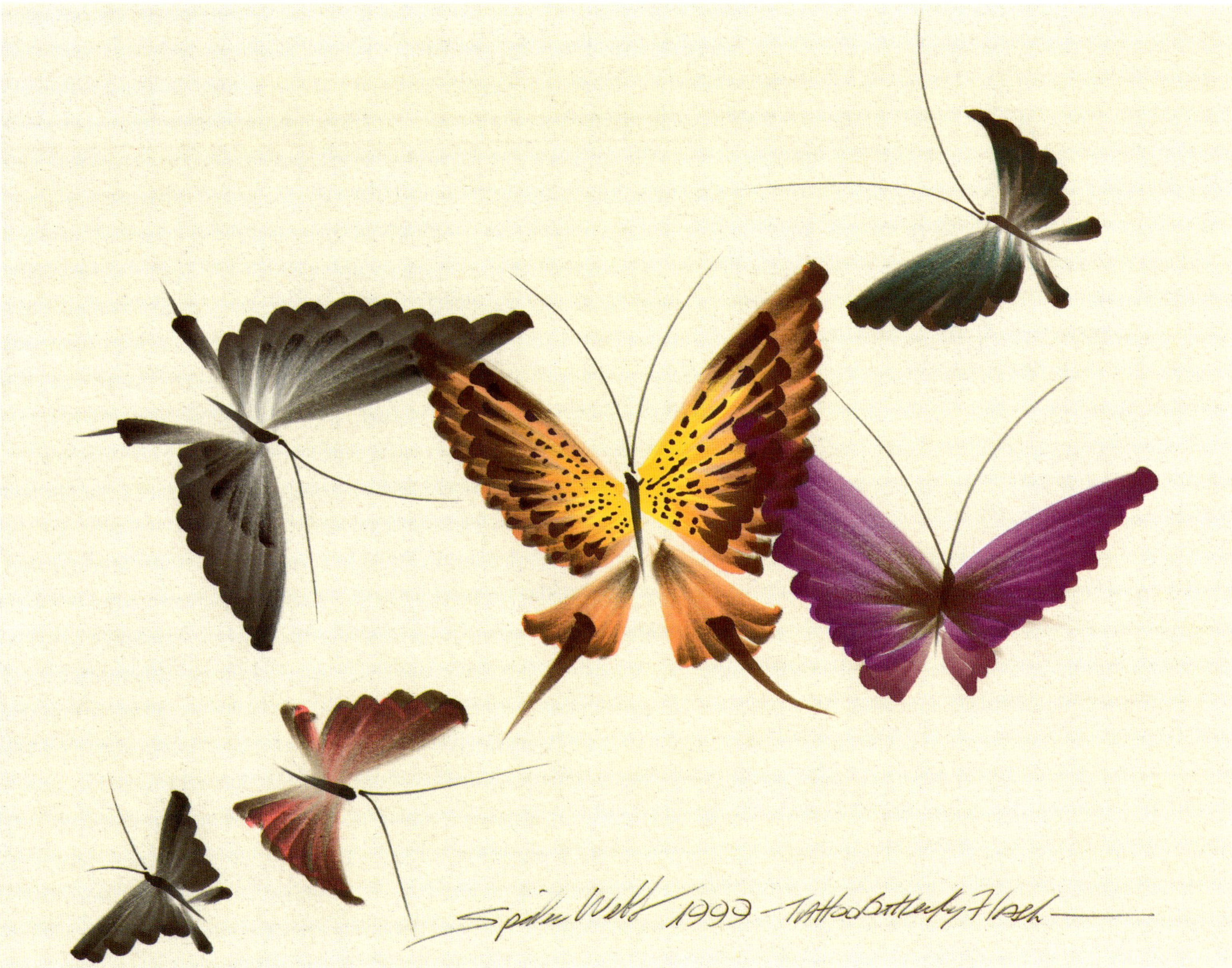
Spider Webb 1999 - Tattoo Butterfly Flash

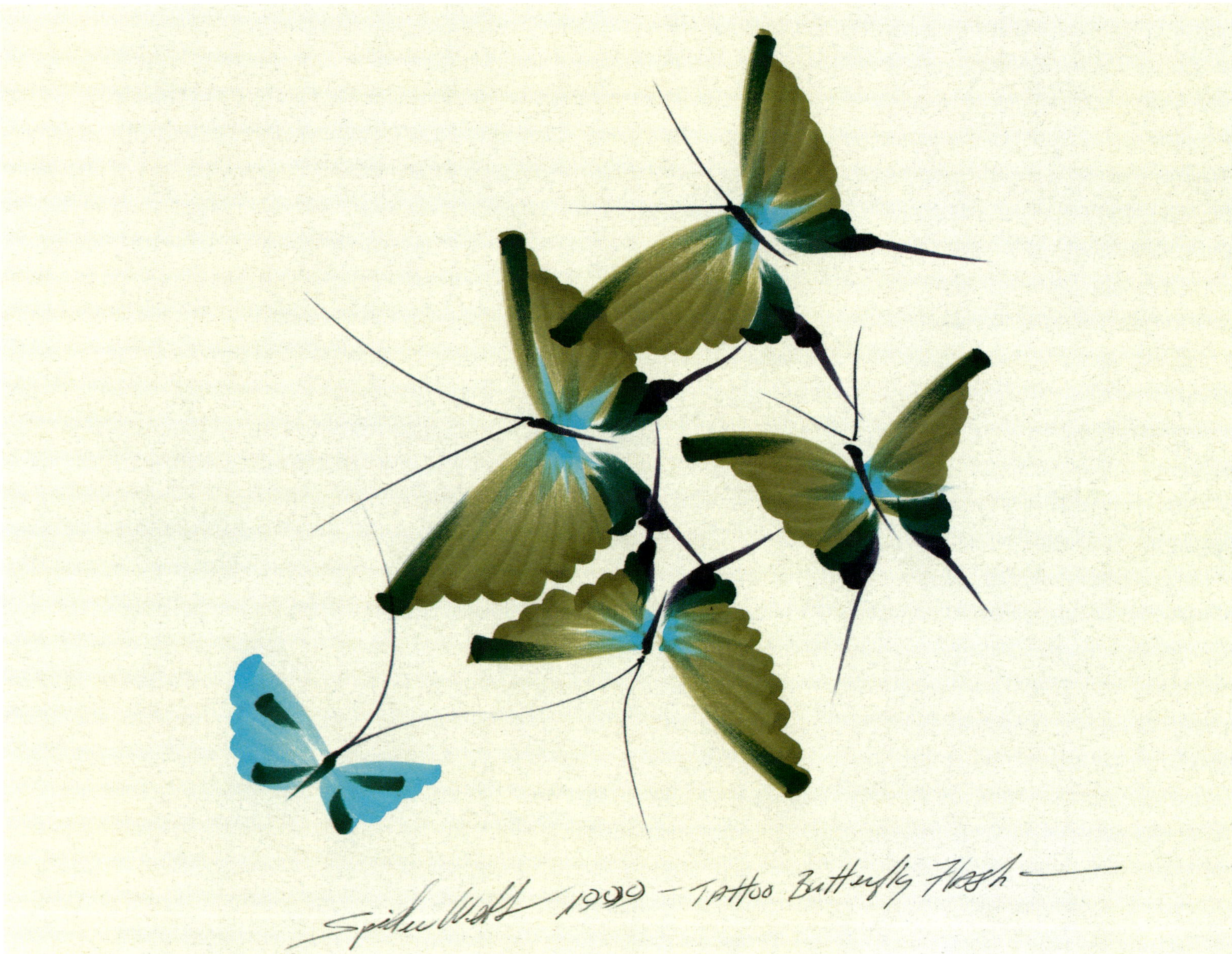
Spider Webb 1999 - TAttoo Butterfly Flash

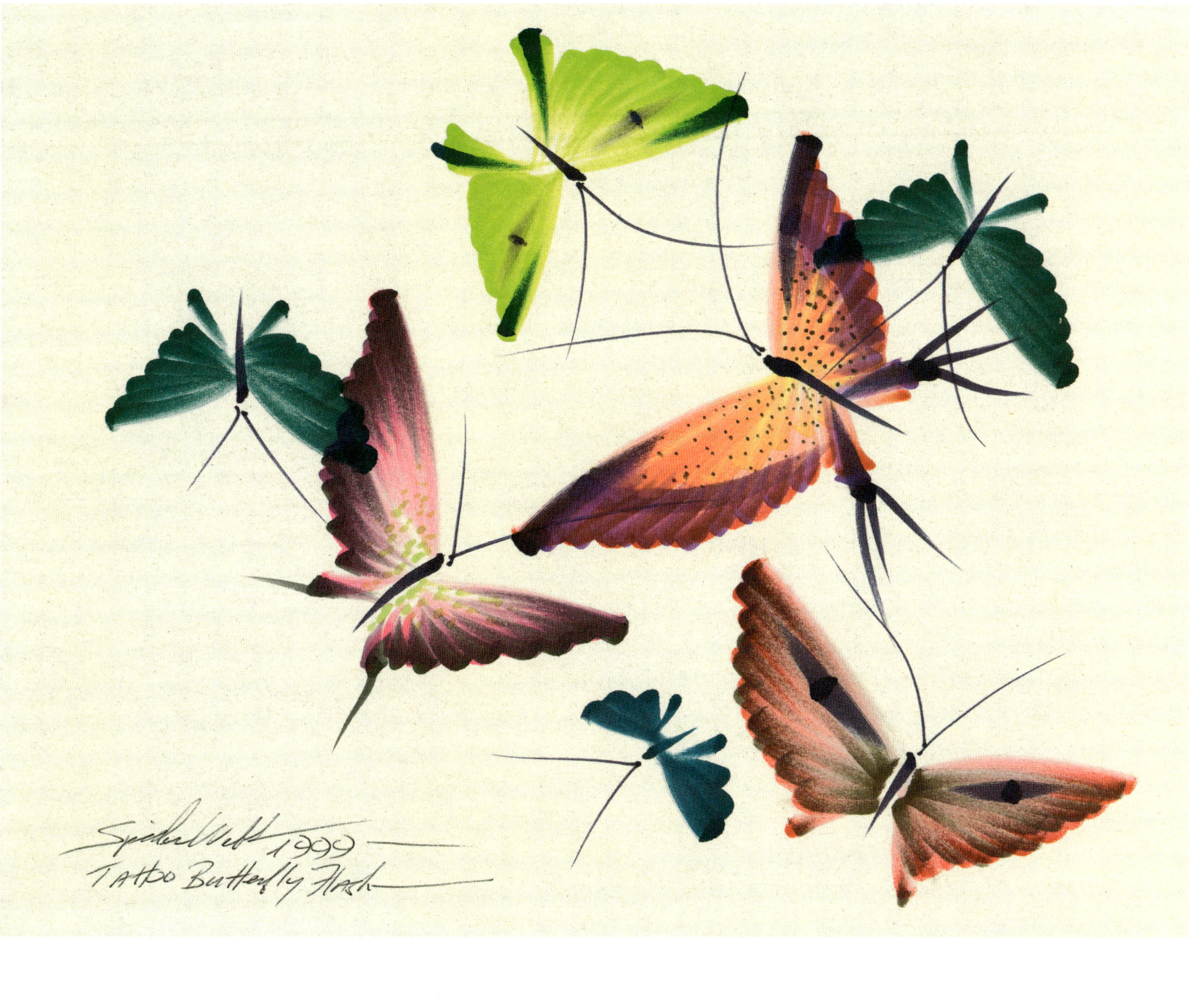
Spider Webb 1999
TAttoo Butterfly Flash

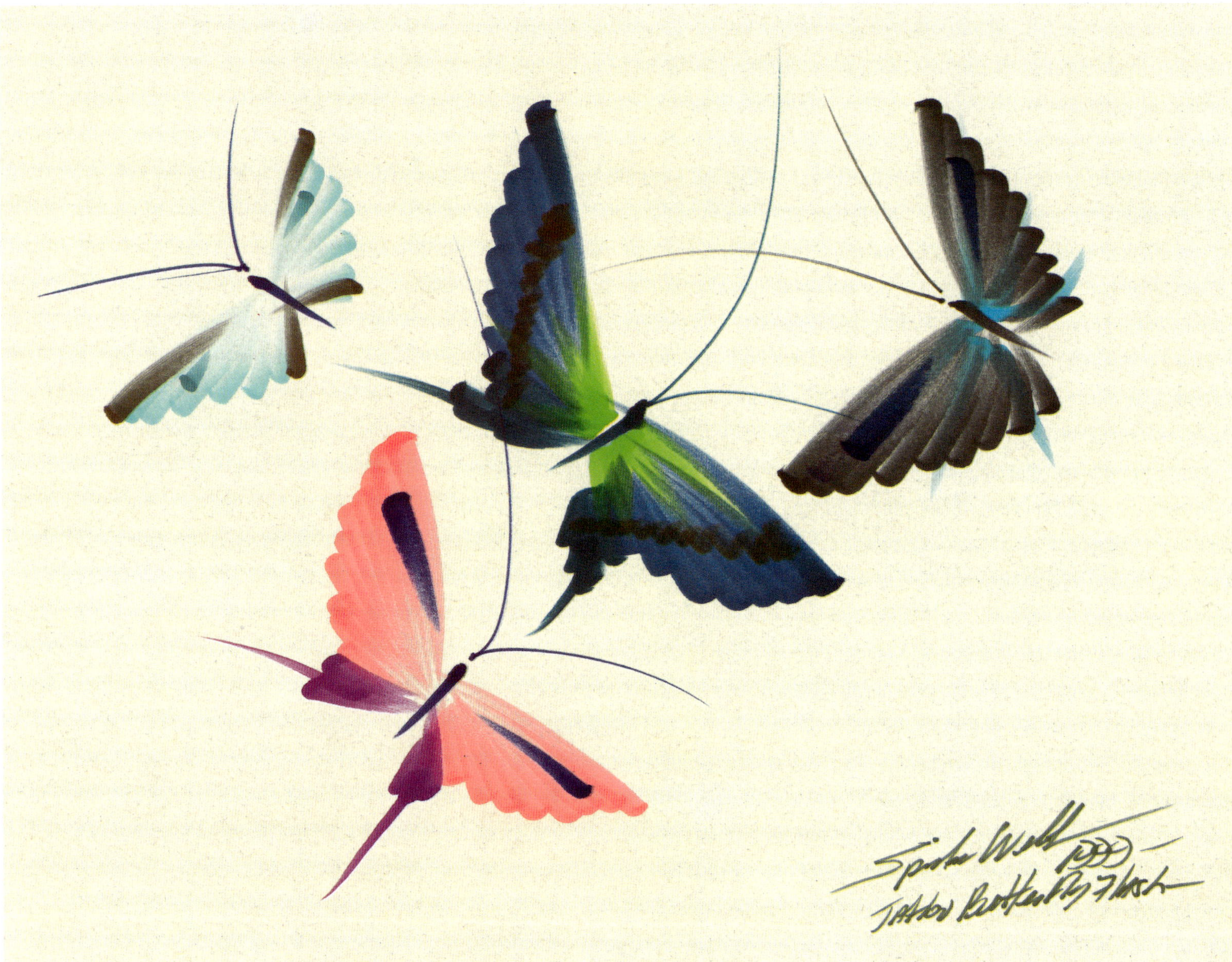

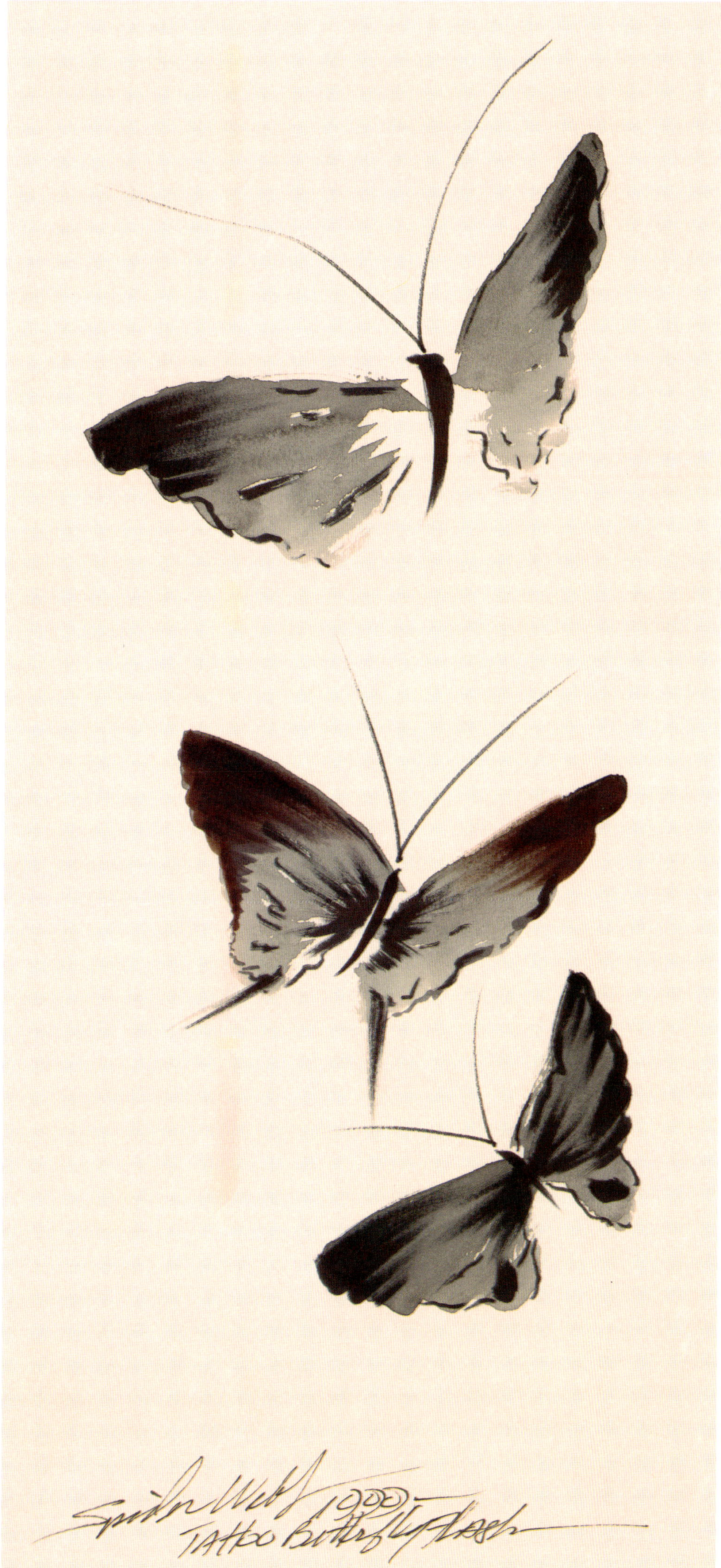
Spider Webb
Tattoo Butterfly Flash

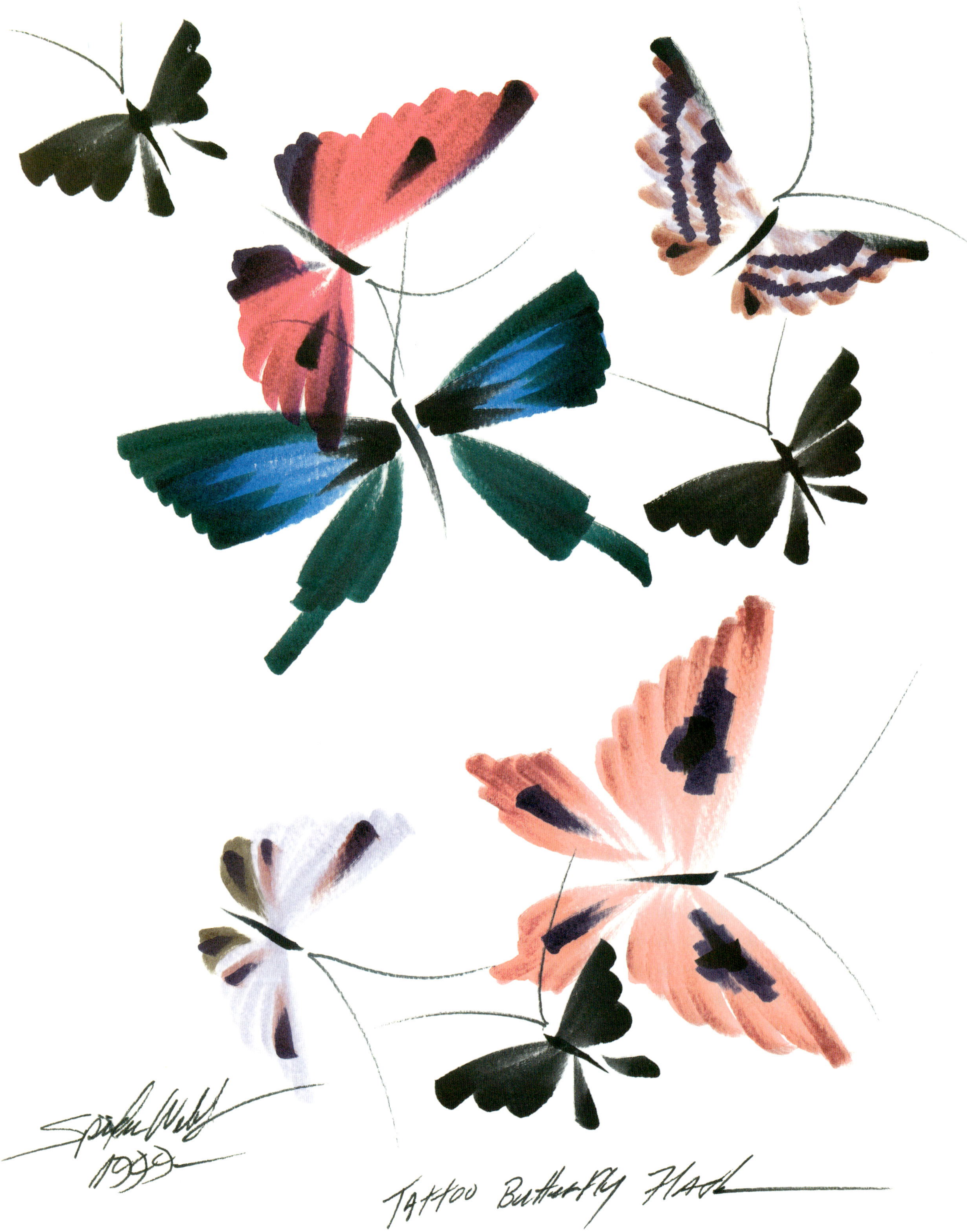
Tattoo Butterfly Flash

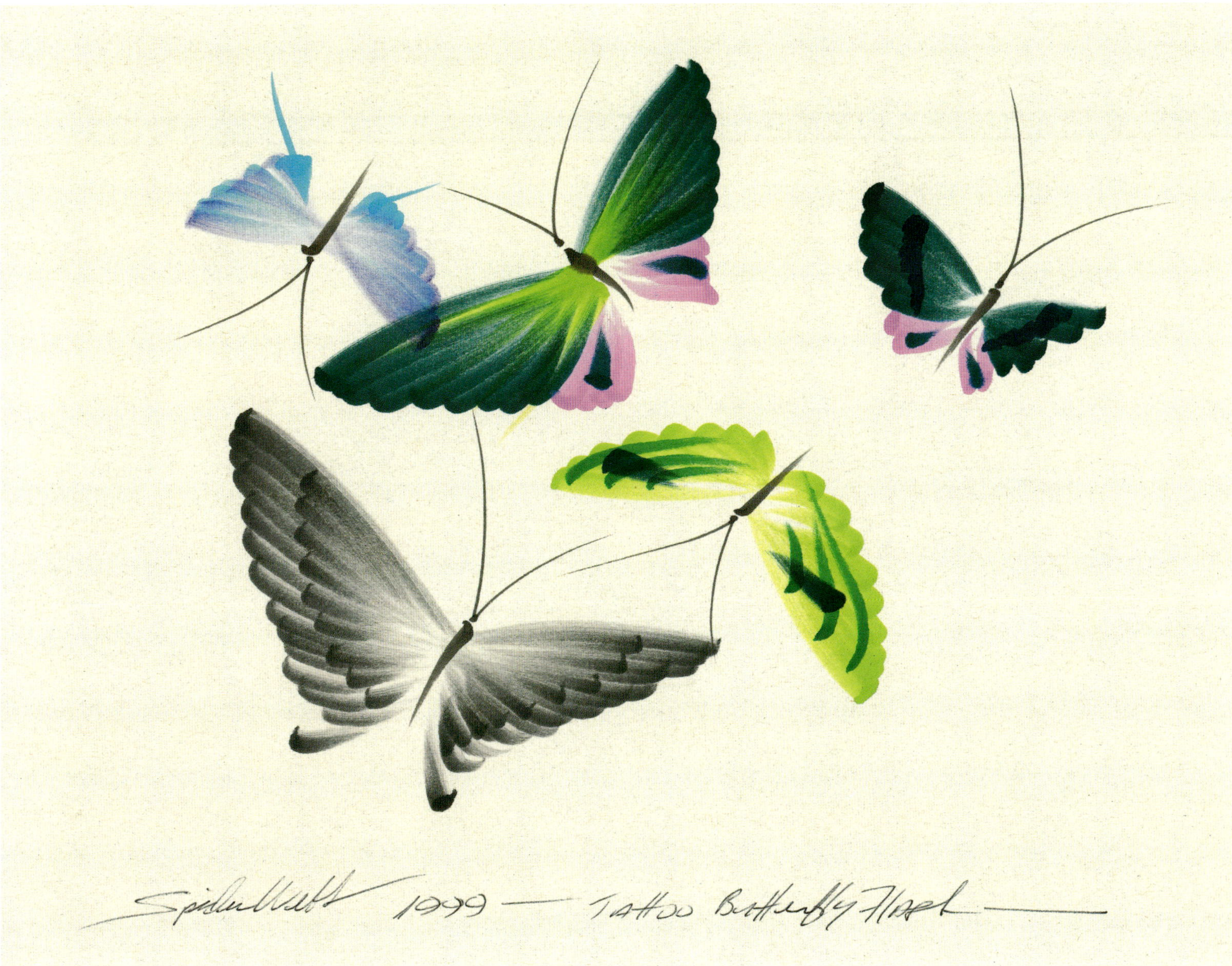
Spider Webb 1999 — Tattoo Butterfly Flash

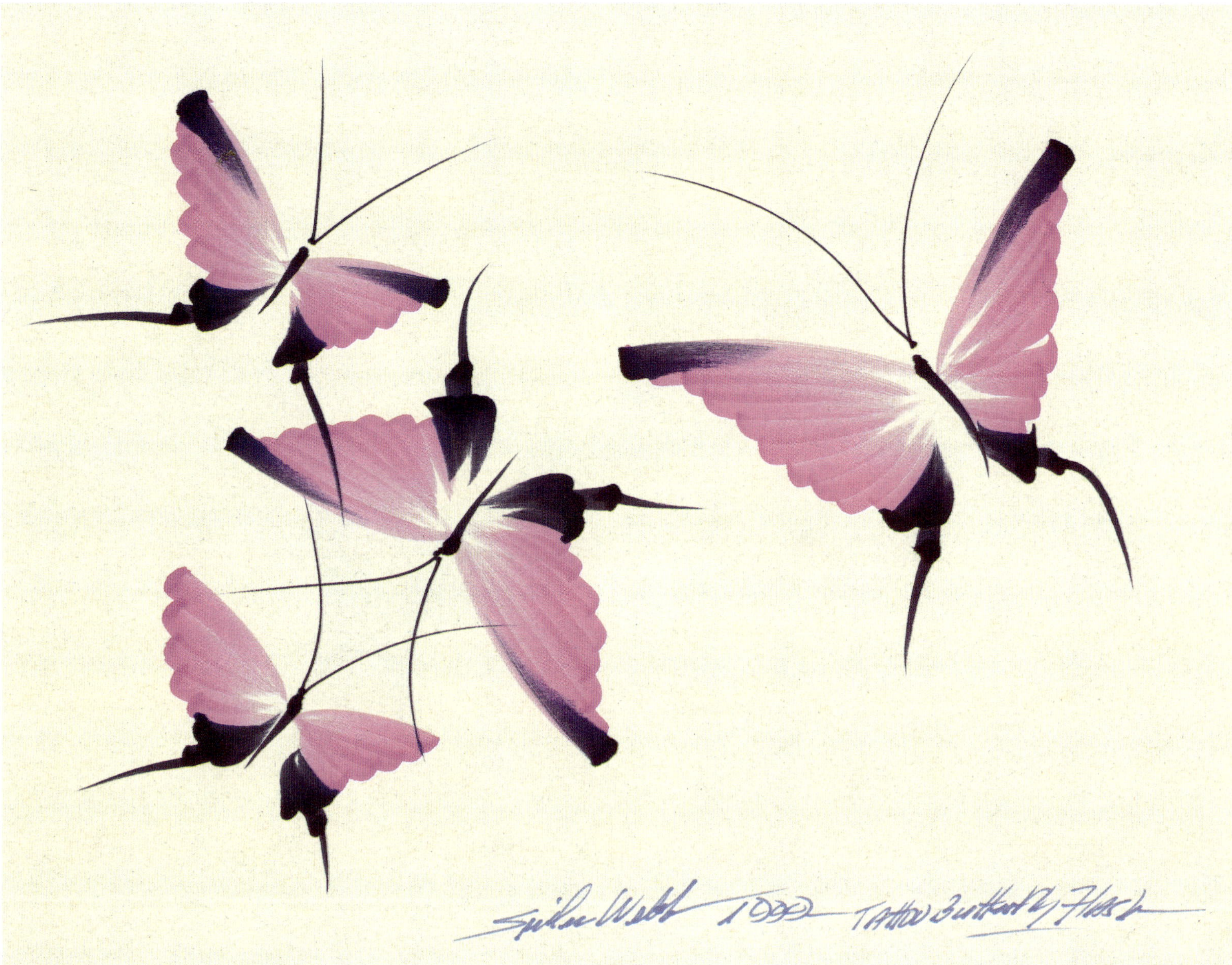

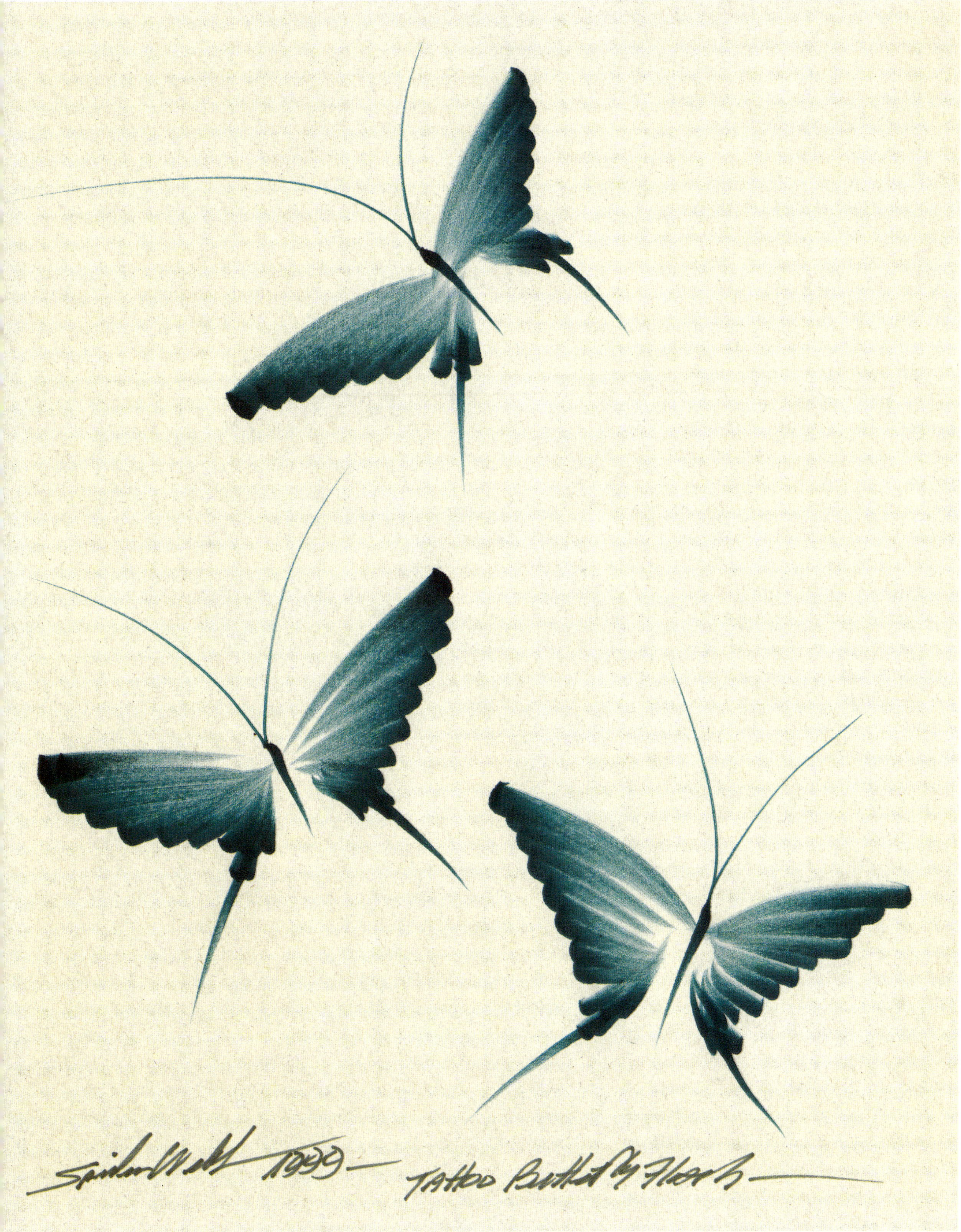
1999

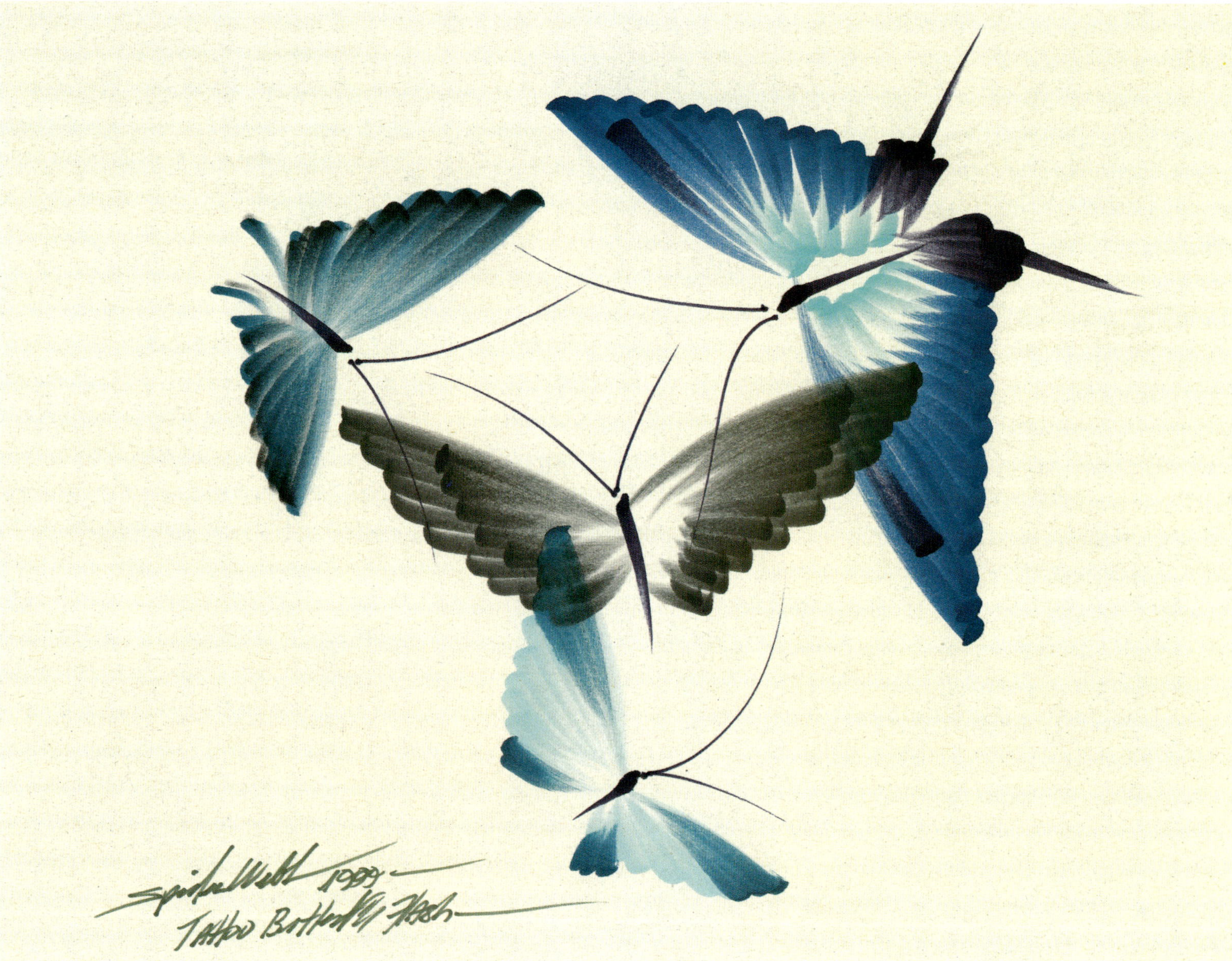
1989
Tattoo Butterfly Flash

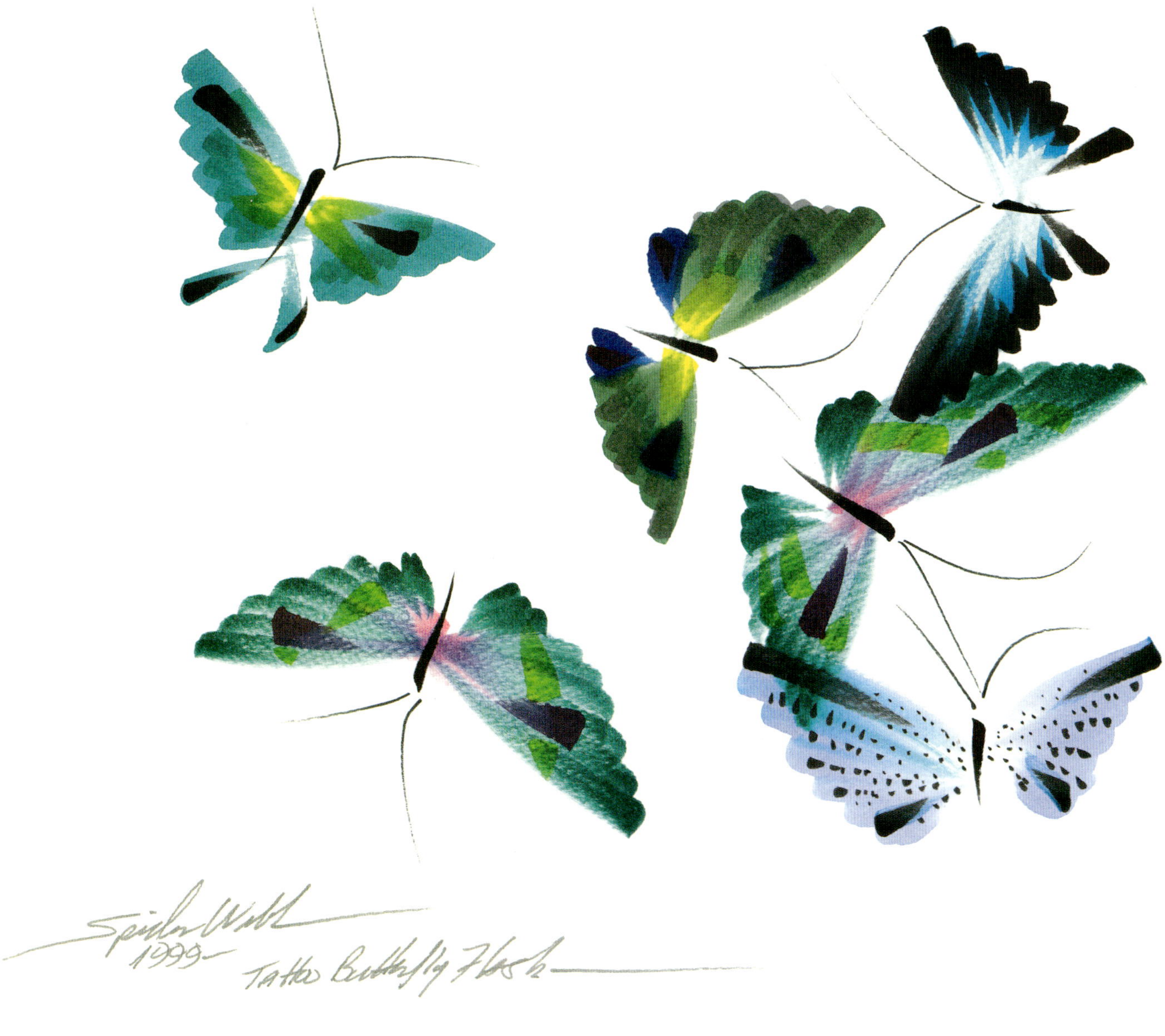
Spider Webb
1999
Tattoo Butterfly Flash

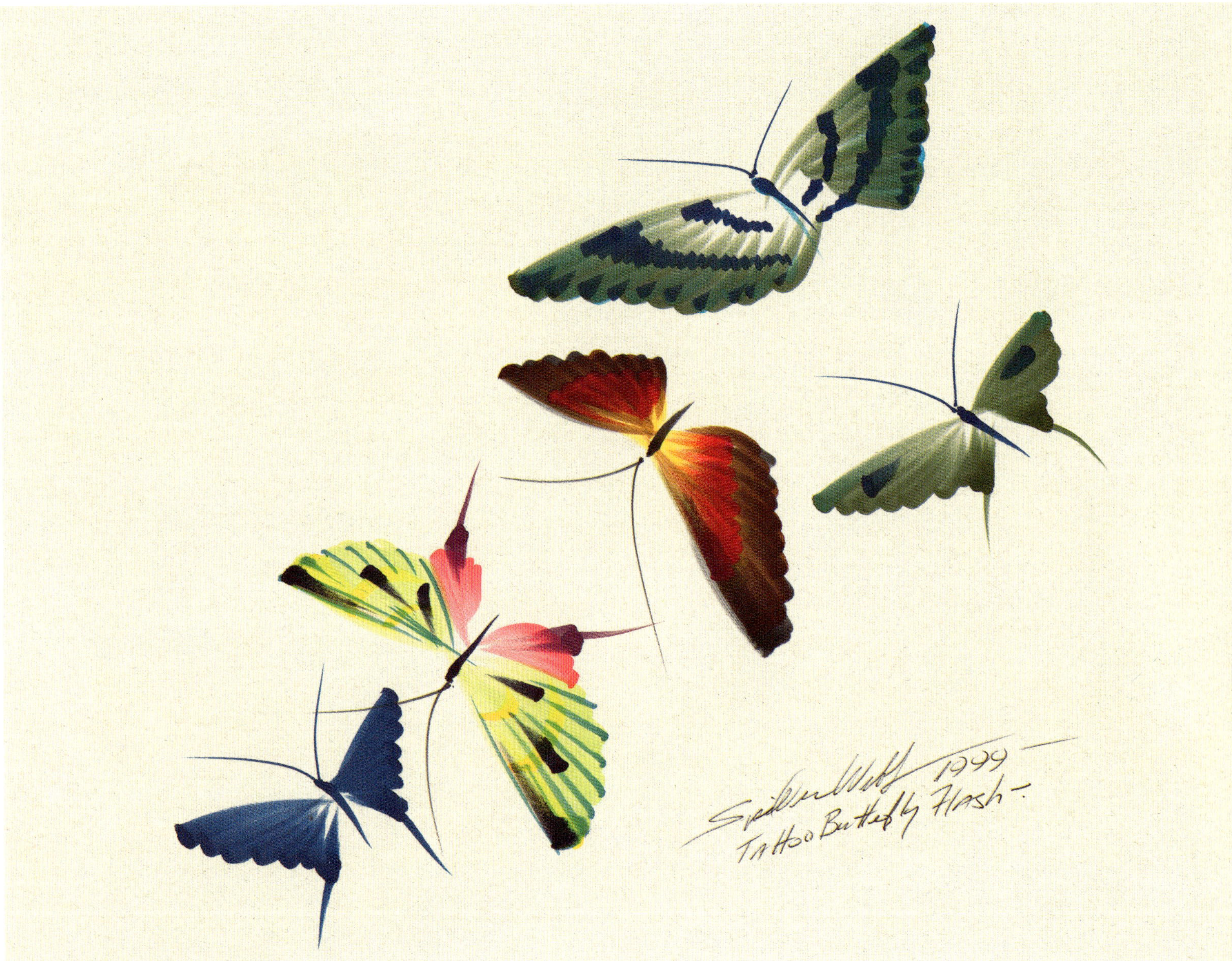
1999
Tattoo Butterfly Flash

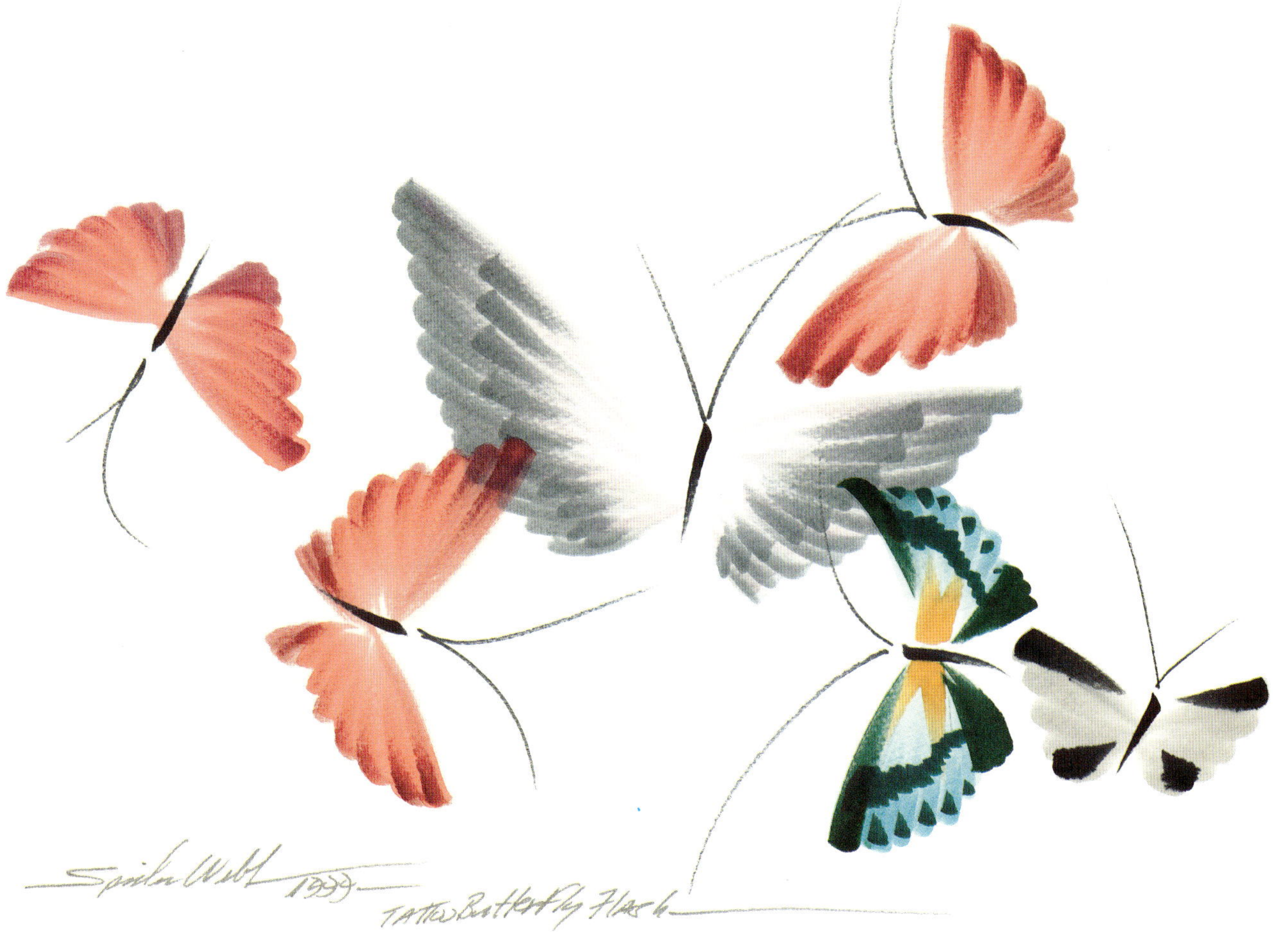
Spider Webb 1999
Tattoo Butterfly Flash

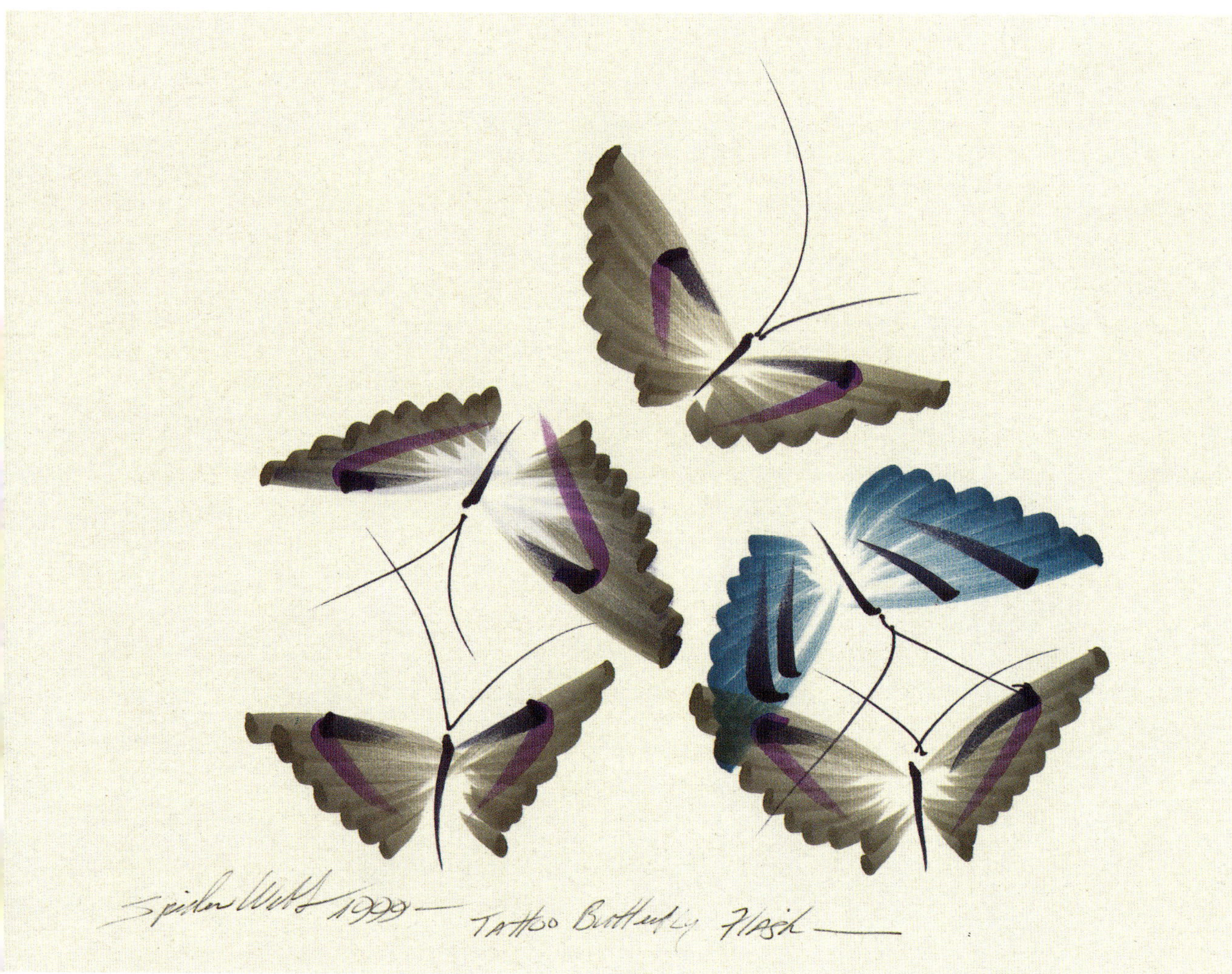
Spider Webb 1999
Tattoo Butterfly Flash

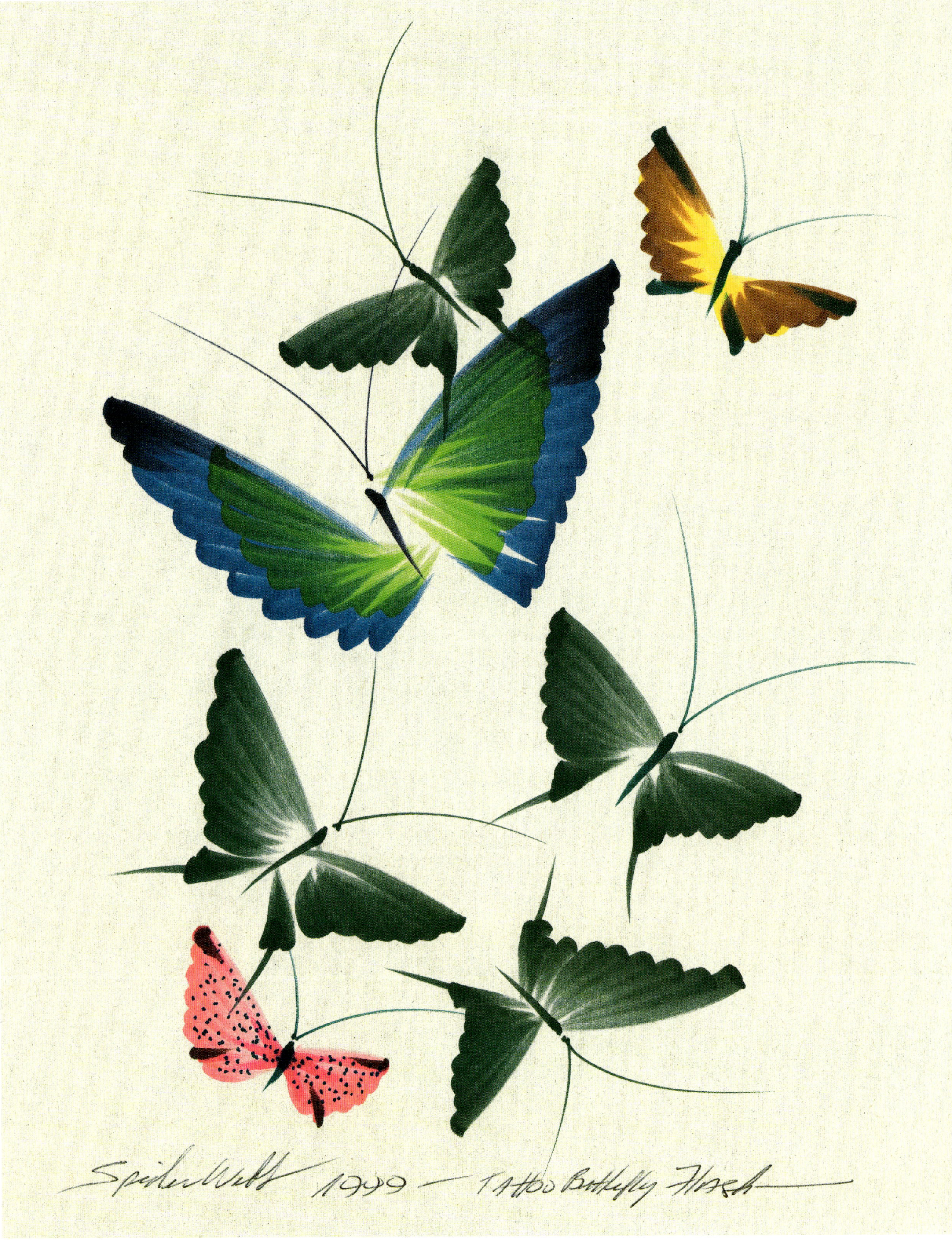
Spider Webb 1999 — TAttoo Butterfly Flash